Methods in Action

Study Guide and Activities Workbook

for

Ray's

Methods Toward a Science of Behavior and Experience

Eighth Edition

Lynnette C. Zelezny, Ph. D.
California State University, Fresno

THOMSON

WADSWORTH

Australia • Brazil • Canada • Mexico • Singapore • Spain • United Kingdom • United States

Printer: EPAC Technologies, Inc.

0-495-03105-4

Cover Image: © Luis Alonso Ocana/age fotostock

Thomson Higher Education
10 Davis Drive
Belmont, CA 94002-3098
USA

For more information about our products,
contact us at:
Thomson Learning Academic Resource Center
1-800-423-0563

For permission to use material from this text or product, submit a request online at
http://www.thomsonrights.com.
Any additional questions about permissions can be submitted by email to **thomsonrights@thomson.com.**

To my children,

Serena, Reed, and Stephen Zelezny,

and to my students

from whom I've learned so very much.

CONTENTS

Chapter 1   What is Science?   **1**

Chapter Objectives: Concept Checks   1

Study guide and Review   2
  Key Terms   2
  Fill-in: Self Test   3
  True/False: Self Test   4
  Multiple Choice: Self Test   4
  Essays   7

Research Activities   10
  1. Insanity Plea: Inferring Subjective Experience in Science   10
  2. Science in the Media   11
  3. Who is Smarter, Girls or boys? Tenacity Statements   11
  4. Ted Bundy: Porn Addict and Serial Killer. Questioning Authority   11

Research Summary and Discussion Questions   12
  Science and Antiscience
  by W. R. Brain

Question Answers   13

Chapter 2   Methods of Science   **14**

Chapter Objectives: Concept Checks   14

Study guide and Review   15
  Key Terms   15
  Fill-in: Self Test   16
  True/False: Self Test   17
  Multiple Choice: Self Test   18
  Essays   20

Research Activities   23
  1. Altruism Research: Library Research   23
  2. Children and Shyness: Naturalistic Observation   23
  3. Pace of Life: Naturalistic Observation   24
  4. Graffiti in Public Restrooms: Naturalistic Study   24

Research Summary and Discussion Questions   25
  The Nature of Love
  by H. Harlow

Suggested Readings   26

Question Answers   27

Chapter 3   **Developing the Hypothesis**   29

  Chapter Objectives: Concept Checks   29

  Study guide and Review   30
   Key Terms   30
   Fill-in: Self Test   31
   True/False: Self Test   32
   Multiple Choice: Self Test   33
   Essays   36

  Research Activities   37
   1. Mapping Out Research Ideas   37
   2. Daily Journal of Research Ideas   37
   3. Gaining Library Skills   37
   4. Depression Among College Students: Developing Hypotheses   38
   5. Empirical Test of Clichés   38
   6. Finding Psychological Articles and Tests on the Internet   38

  Research Summary and Discussion Questions   39
   Bystander Intervention in Emergencies: Diffusion of Responsibility
   by J. Darley, & B. Latane

  Suggested Readings   39

  Question Answers   40

Chapter 4   **Description of Behavior: Numerical Representation**   42

  Chapter Objectives: Concept Checks   42

  Study guide and Review   43
   Key Terms   43
   Fill-in: Self Test   45
   True/False: Self Test   46
   Multiple Choice: Self Test   47
   Essays   51

  Research Activities   53
   1. Physical Activity and Mood: Correlational Study   53
   2. Parents, Sexual Information and Risk Taking Behaviors: 54
      Correlational Study
   3. Assess Your Self-Esteem   55

  Research Summary and Discussion Questions   57
   The Social Adjustment Rating Scale
   by T. H. Holmes, & R. H Rahne

  Suggested Readings   58

  Question Answers   58

Chapter 5   Inferential Statistics   **60**

Chapter Objectives: Concept Checks   60

Study guide and Review   61
Key Terms   61
Fill-in: Self Test   62
True/False: Self Test   63
Multiple Choice: Self Test   64
Essays   66

Research Activities   67
1. Sports Psychology: Improving Athletic Performance with Mental Imagery   67
2. Sex-typing of Infants: Analysis using t-tests   67
   a. Design a Flowchart   72
   b. Write an APA Abstract   72
3. Mozart and Baby IQ: Identify Threats to Validity   73

Research Summary and Discussion Questions   74
The Effect of Choice and Enhanced Personal Responsibility for the Aged by E. Langer, & J. Rodin

Suggested Readings   74

Question Answers   75

Chapter 6   Testing Hypothesis   **76**

Chapter Objectives: Concept Checks   76

Study guide and Review   77
Key Terms   77
Fill-in: Self Test   78
True/False: Self Test   80
Multiple Choice: Self Test   81
Essays   84

Research Activities   85
1. TV Violence and Aggression: Develop a Research Hypothesis   85
2. Identify the Confounds   85
   a. Mountain Climbing and Perceived Competence   85
   b. REM Deprivation and Mazes   85
   c. Anti-smoking Interventions for Sixth Graders   86
   d. Teen Sex Interventions   86
3. Identifying Type I and Type II Errors   86
   a. AIDS Vaccine   86
   b. Competitive vs. Cooperative Learning   86
   c. Silicon Breast Implants   87
   d. Lobotomies to Cure Depression   87

Research Summary and Discussion Questions   88
  The "Visual Cliff"
  by E. Gibson, & R. Walk

Suggested Readings   88

Question Answers   89

Chapter 7   Control   **91**

Chapter Objectives: Concept Checks   91

Study guide and Review   92
  Key Terms   92
  Fill-in: Self Test   93
  True/False: Self Test   94
  Multiple Choice: Self Test   95
  Essays   98

Research Activities   98
  1. Design a Research Flowchart   98
  2. Anorexic Patients: Random Assignment using a Random Number Table   99
  3. Identifying Experimental Designs   103
    a. Caffeine and PMS   103
    b. Computers, Visualization and T-cell Production in Cancer Patients   103
    c. Positive Self Statements, Self Esteem and Battered Woman's Syndrome   103
  4. Improving Pro-environmental Behaviors of Students   104

Research Summary and Discussion Questions   104
  Cognitive Consequences of Forced Compliance
  by L. Festinger, & J. Carlsmith

Suggested Readings   105

Question Answers   105

Chapter 8   Between-Subjects Design   **107**

Chapter Objectives: Concept Checks   107

Study guide and Review   108
  Key Terms   108
  Fill-in: Self Test   109
  True/False: Self Test   110
  Multiple Choice: Self Test   111
  Essays   114

Research Activities   114
  1. Dirty Words, Alcohol and Memory. Factorial Analysis of Variance   114
  2. Fasting and Meditation Effects on Spiritual Awareness. Factorial Study   116
  3. Predicting Main Effects and Interactions in Factorial Designs   117

Research Summary and Discussion Questions   117
Transmission of Aggression through Imitation of Aggressive Models
by A. Bandura, D. Ross, & S. A. Ross

Suggested Readings   118

Question Answers   119

Chapter 9   Within Subjects and Matched Designs   **121**

Chapter Objectives: Concept Checks   121

Study guide and Review   122
  Key Terms   122
  Fill-in: Self Test   123
  True/False: Self Test   124
  Multiple Choice: Self Test   125
  Essays   127

Research Activities   128
  1. Marriage Enrichment Participants: Matching   128
  2. Identifying Experimental Designs   129
    a. Goal Setting and Work Productivity   129
    b. Maternal Touching and Antisocial Behavior in Chimps   130
    c. Just Say No! Contracts and Teen Drunk Driving   130
  3. Hyperactive Children and Effective Interventions: Carryover Effects   131
  4. Japanese vs. American Students on Math/Science Competence   131
  5. Memory and Music. Repeated Measures vs. Between Subjects Design   132

Research Summary and Discussion Questions   132
Opinions and Social Pressure
by S. Asch

Question Answers   133

Chapter 10   Ecology of the Experiment   **134**

Chapter Objectives: Concept Checks   134

Study guide and Review   135
  Key Terms   135
  Fill-in: Self Test   136
  True/False: Self Test   137
  Multiple Choice: Self Test   138
  Essays   141

Research Activities   142
  1. The Volunteer Bias   142
  2. Violence on Network News: Content Analysis   143
  3. Calculate Interrater Reliability   143
  4. Obesity, Weight Loss and Experimenter Effects   144
  5. Culture and Social Bias   144

Research Summary and Discussion Questions   145
Teachers' Expectancies: Determinate of Pupil's IQ Gains
by R. Rosenthal, & L. Jacobson

Suggested Readings   145

Question Answers   145

Chapter 11   Quasi-Experimental and Correlational Designs   **147**

Chapter Objectives: Concept Checks   147

Study guide and Review   148
  Key Terms   148
  Fill-in: Self Test   149
  True/False: Self Test   150
  Multiple Choice: Self Test   151
  Essays   153

Research Activities   154
  1. Gender and Helping Behavior. Conduct a Quasi-Experimental Study   154
  2. Happiness, Financial Wealth and Marital Status: Correlational Study   155
  3. Effect of Three Strikes Law on Crime: Interrupted Time Series   157

Research Summary and Discussion Questions   158
  Birth Order and Intellectual Development
  by R. Zajonc, & G. Markus

Suggested Readings   158

Question Answers   159

Chapter 12   Single Subject Designs   **161**

Chapter Objectives: Concept Checks   161

Study guide and Review   162
  Key Terms   162
  Fill-in: Self Test   163
  True/False: Self Test   164
  Multiple Choice: Self Test   165
  Essays   168

Research Activities   169
  1. Design a Multiple Baseline Study   169
    a. Multiple Phobias and Systematic Desensitization   169
    b. Autism and Self Abusive Behavior   169
  2. Reinforcement of Prosocial Behavior: Reversal Design   169
  3. Dreams: Personal Case Study   173

Research Summary and Discussion Questions   174
  Effect of Dream Deprivation
  by W. Dement

Suggested Readings   174

Question Answers   175

Chapter 13   Questionnaires, Surveys, and Sampling   177

  Chapter Objectives: Concept Checks   177

  Study guide and Review   177
    Key Terms   177
    Fill-in: Self Test   179
    True/False: Self Test   180
    Multiple Choice: Self Test   181
    Essays   185

  Research Activities   187
    1. Minority Attitudes on Controversial Legislation   187
    2. Gallup Polls: Internet Search   187
    3. AIDS Attitudes. Design a Questionnaire   187
    4. Debate Hite's Survey Research   188
    5. Death with Dignity: Conduct a Survey   189

  Research Summary and Discussion Questions   192
    Women and Love
    by S. Hite

  Suggested Readings   192

  Question Answers   193

Chapter 14   Ethics   **195**

  Chapter Objectives: Concept Checks   195

  Study guide and Review   196
    Key Terms   196
    Fill-in: Self Test   197
    True/False: Self Test   198
    Multiple Choice: Self Test   199
    Essays   203

  Research Activities   204
    1. Debate the Tea Room Trade Study   204
    2. Develop an Informed Consent   204
    3. Animal Subjects in Research   206
    4. Stanford Prison Study   206

Research Summary and Discussion Questions   207
    Behavioral Study of Obedience
    by S. Milgram

Suggested Readings   207

Question Answers   208

Chapter 15   Sharing Results   210

Chapter Objectives: Concept Checks   210

Study guide and Review   211
  Key Terms   211
  Fill-in: Self Test   212
  True/False: Self Test   213
  Multiple Choice: Self Test   214
  Essays   217

Research Activities   218
  1. Correct APA Format   218
  2. Critique an APA Article   219
  3. Write a Research Proposal   220
  4. Romantic Interpersonal Relationships: Peer Review   221

Research Summary and Discussion Questions   222
  What goes where? An activity to teach the organization of journal articles.
  by R. Ault

Suggested Readings   222

Question Answers   222

Chapter 16   Beyond Method   224
Chapter Objectives: Concept Checks   224

Study guide and Review   225
  Key Terms   225
  Fill-in: Self Test   226
  True/False: Self Test   226
  Multiple Choice: Self Test   227
  Essays   230

Research Activities   230
  1. Developing Futuristic Research Questions   230
  2. Cross Cultural Sexuality Research. Is Science Value Free?   230

Research Summary and Discussion Questions   231
  Constants Across Cultures in the Face and Emotion
  by P. Ekman, & W. Friesen

Suggested Readings   231

Question Answers   232

Acknowledgments

My thanks to
Michael E. Olsen,
California State University, Fresno,
for his exemplary research assistance
on this book.

CHAPTER 1

What Is Science?

CHAPTER OBJECTIVES: CONCEPT CHECKS

The chapter objectives provide you with a concept checklist. These are things you should know after reading Chapter 1. The accompanying text page numbers are reference aids for your review.

1. What roles do the scientist, research participant, and witness play in science? (3)

2. Compare and contrast the different methods of knowing: tenacity, authority, reason, common sense, and science. (4-7)

3. How did Galileo advance our thinking from authority to empiricism? (5)

4. What important strides did Croesus, Galen, and Semmelweis make? How have we advanced in our contemporary scientific approach? (8-13)

5. What are the major characteristics of the scientific approach? (7)

6. Why are scientific conclusions never considered final? (14-15)

7. What is the importance of replication in science? How is replication part of the feedback component in science? (10)

8. Explain how the scientific method's feedback component refines ideas. (7)

9. What are Newton's Rules of Reasoning (1680) and how are they still utilized today by scientists? (8-9)

10. How does the concept of empiricism relate to our study of behavior and experience? (14)

11. Summarize Schumacher's four ways of studying psychological processes. (15-17)

12. How is psychology like other sciences in its reliance on objective observation to study indirectly unobservable phenomena? (20)

STUDY GUIDE AND REVIEW

<u>**Key Terms**</u>

Define each of these terms in your own words. Check your understanding of Chapter 1 by referring to the featured text page.

1. Methods of knowing:

    a. Tenacity (4)

    b. Authority (4)

    c. Reason (5-6)

    d. Common sense (6)

    e. Science (6-7)

2. Operational definitions (7)

3. Law of parsimony (8)

4. Natural order (8)

5. Verifiable through experience (7)

6. Universal (8-9)

7. Replication (10)

8. Empiricism (14)

9. Objective (15)

10. Behavior (15)

11. Experience (15)

12. Marker variable (17)

13. Inference (19)

14. Construct (19)

Fill-in: Self Test

Fill in the missing word or phrase. Focus your attention on important Chapter 1 details.

1. _____ is a valuable tool in bridging the gap between ideas and real life that is basic to all research strategies. (2)

2. General scientific conclusions drawn from observations are called _____. (2)

3. An important point about scientific facts is that they must be assessed in terms of their human value. This is the _____ approach to scientific understanding. (2)

4. A belief that is presented over and over and accepted as truth is characteristic of _____. (4)

5. A(n) _____ specifies what is to be measured and how it is to be measured. (7)

6. Scientific conclusions are never taken as final but are always open to _____ as new information is evaluated. (9)

7. Natural events should be explained in the simplest possible way. This is based on Newton's _____. (8)

8. A major characteristic of science is its reliance on information that is _____ through experience. (7)

9. The early approaches by Croesus, Galen, and Semmelweis were important because the manner in which they sought solutions represented a(n) _____ process. (11)

10. Croesus was methodical in his information gathering, but he had not learned the role of _____ in science. (9)

11. _____ is a process of relying on sensory experience to verify our ideas about reality. (14)

12. A(n) _____ is a concept used in a theoretical manner that ties together a number of observations. (19)

13. A feature common to all science is its reliance on _____ observation to study indirectly unobservable phenomena. (19)

True/False: Self Test

Test your understanding of Chapter 1 by marking the best answer to these true or false items.

1. _____ It is possible to have perfect logic but an inaccurate original assumption. (5-6)

2. _____ Reason is an improvement over tenacity and authority because it utilizes experience. (6)

3. _____ Unlike common sense, science verifies observation by replication. (6)

4. _____ Galen's work illustrates the importance of going past observations; however, he failed to examine alternatives. (10)

5. _____ Psychology incorporates traditional objective observation but is unique in its attempt to study indirectly unobservable phenomena. (19)

6. _____ Authority brings stability and allows for consistency; however, it is important to examine the basis of the authority's claim. (4)

7. _____ Once a statement is based solely on tenacity and is widely accepted, it is not very difficult to change. (4)

8. _____ There is no single scientific method. (2)

9. _____ Known facts about a particular subject are called scientific knowledge (3)

10. _____ Three actors in the drama of science are the scientist, research participant, and witness. (3)

Multiple Choice: Self Test

Test your Chapter 1 comprehension by circling the best answer to these multiple choice questions.

1. "Girls aren't good at math" is an example of an empty phrase that is repeatedly presented. This exemplifies _____. (4)

   a. Common sense
   b. Tenacity
   c. Science
   d. Authority

2. How is the method of tenacity limiting? (4)

   a. Facts must be viewed in light of human value.
   b. Facts are sometimes descriptive and can be represented only by numbers.
   c. The accuracy of belief may never have been evaluated.
   d. All of the above

3. Before Galileo, intellectual questions were usually answered by _____. (5)

   a. church authorities
   b. natural science
   c. rules of reason
   d. empiricism

4. Why won't reason alone always produce a valid answer? (6)

   a. Our measuring devices are too limited.
   b. Perfect logic is only a model.
   c. Our original assumptions may be incorrect.
   d. Logical syllogisms are restrictive.

5. In what way does common sense offer an improvement over tenacity, authority, and reason? (6)

    a. It is based on direct evidence.
    b. It uses logical syllogisms.
    c. It applies operational definitions.
    d. Both a and b

6. Based on Alfred North Whitehead's (1925) ideas about science, which of the following is true? (6-7)

    a. Science opens itself to anyone's direct experience.
    b. Science presumes any observation by a scientist can be verified.
    c. Science uses logic and experience to rule out assumptions that do not accurately reflect the real world.
    d. All of the above

7. Science requires which of the following? (2-3)

    a. Doubt
    b. Experience
    c. Refinement
    d. All of the above

8. What is the role of the witness in science? (3)

    a. It relates facts to human concerns.
    b. It defines science in terms of its factual objectivity.
    c. It acts as a feedback component.
    d. It defines scientific conclusions as tentative.

9. Referring to an authority is efficient and beneficial especially if we know nothing about a phenomenon. Which of the following is not an example of referring to an authority? (4)

    a. Voting according to editorial endorsements
    b. Relying on the judgment of your doctor on a serious health care issue
    c. Relying on repeated advertisements in the media
    d. Following the teachings of great religious leaders

10. Which method of knowing is self-corrective? (6-7)

    a. Tenacity
    b. Authority
    c. Common sense
    d. Reason
    e. Science

11. Who is credited as the originator of modern science? (7)

    a. Alfred North Whitehead
    b. Sigmund Freud
    c. Charles Peirce
    d. Isaac Newton
    e. Albert Einstein

12. Traditional psychology asks: How do I study your behavior? According to Schumacher's (1977) schema, what other ways can we study psychological processes? (15-16)

    a. Study one's own inner experience
    b. Study directly the subjective experience of others
    c. Study one's own behavior in terms of how others see it
    d. Both a and c

13. According to the text, what technique is used to infer experience? (18)

    a. Operational biofeedback devices
    b. Role-playing a subject to gain experimental perspective
    c. Create a situation in which different experiences give rise to different behaviors
    d. Both b and c

14. According to the text, which of the following is the most generally true of science? (20)

    a. Science is performed by all people.
    b. Science is a means of excluding our human limitations.
    c. Science accepts it must aim to "prove."
    d. Science does not require support of nor communications with others.

Essays

Apply your knowledge of Chapter 1 as you analyze the following questions in detail. Specifically refer to information in the chapter to support your answers.

1. Why is it a trap to believe that science is the only way of knowing? Address the historical and traditional foundations of science.

2. "The real purpose of the scientific method is to make sure nature hasn't misled you into thinking you know something you don't actually know." - Robert Pirsig

   Discuss the meaning of this quote. Specifically refer to Peirce and the methods of knowing.

3. In Infotrac research phrenology. Do you find the conclusions of phrenologists convincing? Explain why. What criticisms surround this issue? How does phrenology illustrate a limitation of reason?

4. Five Ways of Accepting a Belief: Five statements are presented below. Tell which of the five ways of accepting a belief is reflected by each statement. Which of these statements is most convincing and why?

   a. Vitamin C is part of a healthy diet. Apples contain Vitamin C. Apples should be part of a healthy diet.
   b. The Surgeon General has stated that apples provide many of the nutrients vital to good health.
   c. An apple a day keeps the doctor away.
   d. Apples are natural and nutritious, but cannot be depended on to maintain perfect health.
   e. One medium apple contains 1.42 grams of total dietary fiber and 0.48 grams of cellulose.

5. The text describes four ways of studying psychological processes (presented graphically in Table 1.1). Each of the four summaries below reflects one of these categories. For each, discuss (a) which category the summary best fits and (b) what other research questions you might seek to answer with this approach.

   a. Conway and Ross (1984) studied the way in which people exaggerate the consistency between the way they used to be and the way they currently are. Their study of 106 undergraduates at the beginning and end of a semester implied that whether people perceive stability or change in themselves depends on the cognitive theories they use when reconstructing their past. Conway and Ross found that despite the fact that their grades had not changed, students consistently underestimated their performance at the beginning of the semester (when looking back) to support the invalid theories of change.

   b. Wilhelm Wundt (1862) wanted to scientifically determine the structure of the mind. He set out to do so by studying immediate experiences, without the interference of recording devices. Wundt tried to report sensations as they happened in terms of modality and intensity. The tridimensional theory of feeling, which states that feelings can be described in terms of pleasantness-unpleasantness, excitement-calm, and strain-relaxation, was born out of Wundt's own introspection.

   c. Smith and Sarason (1975) studied 211 college students who were grouped according to their levels of social anxiety (low, moderate, and high). Subjects were asked to role-play a situation in which they were then asked to rate how good or bad the evaluation made them feel; the likelihood that the other student would actually rate that way; and how favorable the other student's evaluation was. Subjects high in social anxiety perceived the same feedback as being more negative than did subjects low in social anxiety. In addition, high social anxiety subjects expected that they would be evaluated negatively. Smith and Sarason suggest that socially anxious persons have negatively biased interpretations of the way in which others view them.

   d. Social facilitation is the tendency for individuals to perform easy tasks more quickly and difficult tasks more slowly in the presence of others. Triplett (1898) studied children in his laboratory. The children were instructed to turn a fishing reel as fast as they could. Triplett found that children turned the reel faster in the presence of other children than they did in the alone condition.

6. Discuss science as an active versus passive enterprise. Explain the role of the scientist, the research participant, and the witness in science.

7. What are Newton's rules of reasoning in science? How do these rules apply to the modern scientific approach?

8. What is empiricism and how has it been used to advance psychology?

9. Compare and contrast the different ways of knowing.

10. How is science limited in measuring questions about life after death?

RESEARCH ACTIVITIES

The goals of the research activities are to: (1) relate Chapter 1 on an applied learning dimension, and (2) get you involved in research.

1. **Insanity Plea: Inferring Subjective Experience in Science.** As discussed in the text, scientists often use objective behavior to study subjective experience. Use Infotrac to find a research article in a psychology journal on the subject of the insanity plea. Address the following below:

   a. Cite the author(s), the year published, the name of the article, the journal, and the page numbers.
   b. What were the research questions?
   c. How did the author use observable behavior to infer insanity? How was insanity measured?
   d. Do you think this was a valid way to measure insanity? If so, what convinced you that it is a valid measure? If not, what would convince you that it was a valid measure?
   e. What conclusions do the investigators reach in this article? How are they tentative or probabilistic? Did the investigators claim they "proved" anything?

2. **Science in the Media.** Science is all around us. Use Infotrac to find a study that uses the scientific method. Identify the research question, how the information was acquired, and what was concluded. Be prepared to report on your research in class and explain what you recognized as the important features of the scientific method.

3. **Who is Smarter, Girls or Boys? Record Statements of Tenacity.** Ask five people these questions: 1) Who is smarter, girls or boys? 2) Why do you think so? Record each statement that is based on tenacity.

    (a) Record the statement.
    (b) Explain if it is widely accepted.
    (c) Discuss in what ways this belief is perpetuated by individuals, the media, or other means.
    (d) How would science address this question?

4. **Ted Bundy. Porn Addict and Serial Killer: Questioning Claims of Authority.**
Go to the library and find this article.

    Ellis-Simons, P. (1989). New hero of a new right: The rising voice of a family
            crusader. *U.S. News & World Report, 106* (5), 27.

This popular psychologist interviewed serial killer, Ted Bundy, before his execution. He attributed Bundy's motivation to kill to his addiction to pornography. Do you agree or disagree with the conclusions of this authority? What other articles can you find on this topic?

5. **Theories.**

    Use InfoTrac to identify a psychological theory. Who developed the theory? Explain the theory. What does it predict?

6. **Women in Science.** Use the internet to find information about women in science over the past 4000 years. **www.astr.ua.edu/4000WS/summary.shtml**

RESEARCH SUMMARY AND DISCUSSION QUESTIONS

What is science?

Brain, W. R. (1965). Science and antiscience. *Science, 145*, 192-197.

In Chapter 1, Ray asks "What is science?" This classic article elaborates on the meaning of science, and addresses science's potential, its challenges, and its responsibilities. The text of this article is from an address to the American Association for the Advancement of Science by a prominent British physician who was the president of the British Association for the Advancement of Science. In his address, Brain called for progress in science. Specifically, he challenged scientists from multiple disciplines to collaborate, and apply scientific knowledge to solve worldwide problems. In conclusion Brain advanced that science has the potential and the responsibility to "unify cultures" and "to achieve a unifying view on which to base a conception of the nature of man."

Discussion Questions:
1. How would you define science?
2. What are some of the misconceptions of science?
3. What world problems might be solved by the application of science?

ANSWERS

Fill-in: Self Test
1. Direct experience
2. Facts
3. Humanistic
4. Tenacity
5. Operational definition
6. Reinterpretation
7. Law of Parsimony
8. Verifiable
9. Systematic
10. Chance
11. Empiricism
12. Construct
13. Objective

True/False: Self Test

1. True
2. False
3. True
4. False
5. False
6. True
7. False
8. True
9. True
10. True

Multiple Choice: Self Test

1. B
2. C
3. A
4. C
5. A
6. D
7. D
8. A
9. C
10. B
11. D
12. D
13. D
14. A

CHAPTER 2

Introduction to the Methods of Science

CHAPTER OBJECTIVES: CONCEPT CHECKS

The chapter objectives provide you with a concept checklist. These are things you should know after reading Chapter 2. The accompanying text page numbers are reference aids for your review.

1. Integrate these three important aspects of science: (1) idea, (2) experience, and (3) reorganization. (25)

2. What are the strengths and weaknesses of naturalistic observation? Give an example of this type of study. (28-30)

3. When would you use the correlational approach? What conclusion is justified? What is a positive correlation? How does it differ from a negative correlation? (30-31)

4. Describe the experimental method. Why is it the most powerful design? Discuss the importance of operational definitions of variables. (32-35)

5. Differentiate between the independent and dependent variables. (34)

6. What is a confounding variable and how does it affect interpretation of the findings? (34-35)

7. Explain causation in terms of necessary and sufficient conditions. (35-36)

8. What is the balance between internal and external validity in research? (38)

9. A scientist relies on both deductive and inductive logic in science. Distinguish between these reasoning methods and evaluate when they are used in the scientific process. (40-41)

10. How does modus tollens apply to testing scientific theories? (43)

11. How are scientists influenced by paradigms? Give examples of paradigm shifts. (45-46)

12. According to the text, what are the four ways to ensure the high quality of research? (46-47)

13. Aristotle emphasized scientific inquiry and argument. How do they relate to communication of science? (47-48)

STUDY GUIDE AND REVIEW

Key Terms

Define each of these terms in your own words. Check your understanding of Chapter 2 by referring to the featured text page.

1. Hypothesis (25)

2. Naturalistic observation (25, 28-30)

3. Correlational approach (26, 30-31)

4. Positive correlation (31)

5. Negative correlation (31)

6. Third variable (31)

7. Experimental method (26, 32-35)

8. Modeling (26)

9. Retrospective methods (27)

10. Experimental group (33)

11. Control group (33)

12. Operational definitions (33)

13. Independent variable (34)

14. Dependent variable (34)

15. Treatment effect (34)

16. Confounding variables (34-35)

17. Causation (35-36)

18. Epistemology (35)

19. Ontology (35)

20. Exploratory research (36-37)

21. Inference (37)

22. Necessary (35)

23. Sufficient (35)

24. Valid (38)

25. Internal validity (38)

26. External validity (38)

27. Generalizability (38)

28. Deduction (39)

29. Induction (39)

30. Modus ponens (42)

31. Affirming the consequent (42)

32. Denying the antecedent (43)

33. Modus tollens (43)

34. Falsification (43)

35. Paradigm (45)

Fill-in: Self Test

Fill in the missing word or phrase. Focus your attention on important Chapter 2 details.

1. An idea that is formally stated as a research question with an expected outcome is called a(n) _____. (25)

2. Scientists seek to draw conclusions or _____ about new ideas. (25)

3. A scientific technique that observes and describes what occurs naturally is called _____. (25)

4. _____ studies identify relationships between two or more variables that can not be manipulated. (30)

5. The variable that the experimenter manipulates is called the _____ variable. (34)

6. The difference in magnitude of the dependent variable between the control and experimental groups is called the _____. (34)

7. _____ designs allow us to investigate the effects of two or more independent variables in the same experiment. (36)

8. _____ means true and capable of being supported. (38)

9. _____ validity refers to applying a particular set of research results to another setting. (38)

10. Studies done in highly controlled and artificial lab settings often cannot be _____ beyond the lab. (38)

11. A valid form of argument, which uses disconfirmatory reasoning, is known as _____. (43)

True/False: Self Test

Test your understanding of Chapter 2 by marking the best answer to these true or false items.

1. _____ Empiricism means accepting sensory information as valid. (25)

2. _____ Few variables are perfectly correlated with one another. (31)

3. _____ A strength of the correlational study is that it determines which variable influences the other variable. (31)

4. _____ You can not demonstrate that one event causes another until you show that there is a high correlation between variables. (31)

5. _____ Correlational studies are often the first step in providing the needed support for later experimental research. (31)

6. _____ Although naturalistic observation is a good way to get a general idea, it is limited in its discovery of significant behavioral patterns. (28-30)

7. _____ The naturalistic approach is most useful for observing the big picture rather than isolated happenings. (28-30)

8. _____ The independent variable is said to be independent because its levels are established by the experimenter after the experiment begins. (34)

9. _____ The dependent variable gets its name because its value depends on the independent variable. (34)

10. _____ A single study can never "prove" a theory is true. (47)

Multiple Choice: Self Test

Test your Chapter 2 comprehension by circling the best answer to these multiple choice questions.

1. When would a correlational approach be scientifically appropriate? (30-31)

    a. When manipulating variables is unethical
    b. When it is impossible or impractical to manipulate variables
    c. When it is necessary to find out how one variable affects another
    d. Both a and b

2. When using the _____ research method the scientist is passive and does not attempt to change the environment; however, when using the _____ research method the scientist is active and structures the activities to study behavior. (28-35)

    a. retrospective, post hoc
    b. qualitative, quantitative
    c. naturalistic, correlational
    d. correlational, experimental
    e. naturalistic, experimental

3. Which of the following is considered a quantitative scientific research method? (28-35)

    a. Naturalistic
    b. Correlational
    c. Experimental
    d. All of the above

4. The behavior the experimenter expects to be affected by the independent variable is the _____. (34)

    a. operational definition
    b. construct
    c. dependent variable
    d. confound

5. If we wanted to know whether a person's health was associated with the number of friends a person had, what type of a research approach would be used?

   a. Naturalistic
   b. Correlational
   c. Modeling
   d. Experimental
   e. All of the above

6. An unspecified variable that may have influenced the two variables in the correlational study is called a(n) _____. (31)

   a. positive correlation
   b. predictor variable
   c. third variable
   d. negative correlation

7. What is necessary for establishing that one variable influences another? (30-31)

   a. Experimental control
   b. Manipulation of the independent variable
   c. High degree of association between the independent and dependent variables
   d. All of the above

8. A process by which we look at evidence available to us and then use our power of reasoning to reach a conclusion defines _____. (42-43)

   a. inference
   b. modus tollens
   c. validity
   d. falsification

9. A scientist must question the validity of conclusions drawn from research. Two major types of validity are _____ and _____. (38)

    a. independent, dependent
    b. treatment, control
    c. internal, external
    d. inductive, deductive
    e. antecedent, consequent

10. A current notion concerning science, which encompasses a philosophical way of seeing the world, refers to _____. (45)

    a. falsification
    b. propositional logic
    c. modus ponens
    d. a paradigm

11. According to Popper, science shows only that a hypothesis has not been proven false. This line of reasoning leads one to conclude that science never _____ a hypothesis. (43-44)

    a. controls
    b. proves
    c. validates
    d. supports

12. Research on the relationship between tobacco use in humans and the incidence of lung cancer provides us with an example of _____. (31)

    a. cause and effect
    b. a positive correlation
    c. a paradigm shift
    d. All of the above

13. Which of the following is considered a quantitative approach to science? (26)

    a. naturalistic observation
    b. correlational design
    c. experimental manipulation
    d. all of the above

14. Which of the following is not a characteristic of naturalistic observation? (28-30)

      a. scientist must control process and flow of events
      b. method emphasizes patterns
      c. most powerful as an exploratory procedure
      d. may not identify causal factors

15. The difference in magnitude of the dependent variable for the control and experimental group is called the _____. (34)

      a. confounding variable
      b. treatment effect
      c. independent variable
      d. operational effect

Essays

Apply your knowledge of Chapter 2 as you analyze the following questions in detail. Specifically refer to information in the chapter to support your answers.

1. As the researcher, you have proposed the hypothesis that exposure of children to television violence is positively related to aggressive behavior. Design a study to test this hypothesis using the correlational approach. Provide operational definitions and describe in detail what your interpretations would be if your results confirmed/did not confirm your hypothesis. In addition, specify any possible third variables that may be operating.

2. September 11, 2001 was a day in history in which thousands of American lives were lost. As a researcher, you investigated and found a positive relationship between altruism and self-efficacy. How do you interpret this finding? Operationally define the two variables used and discuss how changing the definitions may influence the outcome of the study and the conclusions drawn.

3. Research suggests a positive correlation between crime and the number of churches in a city. Interpret this finding. Does this mean that religion somehow causes crime to be higher? Discuss why or why not. Refer to third variables and directionality in your discussion.

4. Using your own ideas, how could you study the behavior of bystanders by using the scientific method? Address the following: hypothesis (expected outcome), variables, operational definitions, and research strategy. See the Suggested Readings list for classic studies by Latane and Darley (1968).

5. Charles Darwin's naturalistic observation of animals in the Galapagos Islands led to the theory of evolution. Describe the four characteristics of the naturalistic approach. Discuss the goals and the role of the scientist.

6. Using your own creativity, operationally define the following variables that may be used in behavioral studies. Specify how you would define these variables, and how you would measure the variables.
   a. stress
   b. success
   c. aggression
   d. intelligence
   e. deprivation

   Share your definition with your class colleagues. Discuss the role of the operational definition. If one study operationally defines a variable differently, does this mean the study will be different in any way? Explain why or why not.

7. Explain how you could justify the following message as an advertiser.

   "Cigarette smoking does not cause cancer in humans."

   Discuss the inappropriate use of the words *cause* and/or *effect* in correlational research.

RESEARCH ACTIVITIES

The goals of the research activities are to: (1) relate Chapter 2 on an applied learning dimension, and (2) get you involved in research.

1. **Altruism Research - - Library Activity.** Go to the library and find two articles on altruism. Answer the following questions separately for each: (a) How was altruism operationally defined? (b) Was the study conducted in the field or a laboratory? (c) Was the study correlational or experimental? (d) What were the author's conclusions? Comment on the generalizability of these findings. See the Suggested Readings list for more on the subject of altruism and the generalizability of this issue (Cialdini & Kenrick, 1976).

2. **Children and Shyness: Design your own research study.** Go to the library and find two research articles on shyness in children. Through examination of the operational definitions and descriptions of shyness within the articles, identify five behaviors that you could observe in a naturalistic study of children on a school playground. Finally, after researching this topic in the library, generate a hypothesis related to shyness. Design a correlational or experimental study that tests this hypothesis.

    Hypothesis checklist: Address the following issues.

    a.   What is the independent variable?
    b.   Is the independent variable manipulated by the investigator?
    c.   What is the dependent variable?
    d.   What outcome are you predicting?
    e   What relationship are you expecting between the variables?
    f.   What types of conclusions will be appropriate?

3. **Pace of Life Research. Naturalistic Observation.** Conduct a naturalistic observational study on the pace of life in your city. Go to a shopping mall or the downtown center of business, and measure the following behaviors: (a) percentage of people wearing watches, (b) walking speed. Begin by operationally defining how you will measure these variables. Next, describe your procedure, that is, how you will collect data. Design a coding sheet for your observations that includes: (a) location, (b) date, (c) time of day you begin and end observation, (d) behaviors to be observed. You may also be interested in demographic information like gender and age. Be observant of patterns and trends. Note any limitations. Was it difficult to remain unobtrusive? Include graphs and tables to illustrate your findings. Be prepared to discuss your findings in class. See the Suggested Readings list for more on Levine's (l990) Pace of Life study.

4. **Graffiti in Public Restrooms. Design a Coding Sheet and Conduct a Naturalistic Study.**
Design a coding sheet that will be used to conduct a naturalistic observation of graffiti
content found in public restrooms. The coding sheet should consist of simple categories
(e.g., sexual versus non-sexual) and more complex categories (e.g., homosexual,
heterosexual and political). Identify the categories as column headings. Observe several
public restrooms for graffiti to collect data. Mark the frequency of observations in each
category. Specify information about the setting (e.g., women's restroom on a university
campus, etc.). Be prepared to discuss your observations in class. Compare the findings of
those who observed male versus female restrooms to determine if the graffiti content is
similar in both settings. Find two research articles that address this issue (See the suggested
reading list).

5. **Media and Violence. Cause and Effect. Research Activity**.
Research InfoTrac to find titles of scientific studies on media and violence. What words
other than cause and effect are used to imply a cause and effect? List three examples.

RESEARCH SUMMARY AND DISCUSSION QUESTIONS

Introduction to the Methods of Science

Harlow H. F. (1958). The nature of love. *American Psychologist, 13*, 673-685.

This study illustrates the essential components of the experimental method. Participants
were randomly assigned to experimental groups, an independent variable was manipulated, a
dependent variable was measured, and variables and experimental procedures were
operationalized as explained in Chapter 2.

Harlow observed that infant rhesus monkeys raised by humans in a laboratory would
cling to cloth in their cages and become highly agitated when the cloth was removed. He
theorized that infant monkeys have a basic need for close contact. Harlow designed an
experiment to test this hypothesis.

Two mechanical surrogate mothers, one with a wire exterior and one with a cloth
exterior, were placed in the cages of infant monkeys. The monkeys were randomly assigned
to experimental conditions. One group was fed by the wire mother and one group was fed by
the cloth mother. Harlow found that, regardless of which surrogate provided nourishment,
all monkeys stayed in close contact with the cloth surrogate. Those monkeys who were fed
by the wire surrogate would leave the cloth surrogate only briefly for nourishment and then
return. Harlow also found that monkeys who were fed by the cloth surrogate had fewer
health problems. Thus, Harlow's research hypothesis was supported.

Discussion Questions

1.   Identify the independent and dependent variables in this study. How was "love" operationally defined?
2.   How were confounding variables controlled for in this study?
3.   Do you think that these findings can be generalized to humans? Explain your answer.

SUGGESTED READINGS

Anderson, S.J., & Verplanck, W.S. (1983). When walls speak. What do they say? *Psychological Record, 3*, 341-359.

Arluke, A., Kutakoff, L., & Levin, J. (1987). Are the times changing? An analysis of gender differences in sexual graffiti. *Sex Roles, 16*, 1-7.

Interesting research on the content of graffiti in public restrooms.

Cialdini, R. B., & Kenrick, D.T. (1976). Altruism as hedonism: A social development perspective on the relationship of negative mood and helping. *Journal of Personality and Social Psychology, 34, 907-914.*

Latane, D., & Darley, J.M. (1968). Group inhibition of bystanders intervention in emergencies. *Journal of Personality and Social Psychology, 10,* 215-221.

Classic research on bystander behavior.

Levine, R. V. (1990, September-October). The pace of life. *American Scientist,* pp. 451-459.

A summary of Levine's work on the pace of life across cities in the U.S. and six other countries. Explains the Pace of Life Index and how measurements were made by the researchers.

ANSWERS

Fill-in: Self Test
1. Hypothesis
2. Inferences
3. Naturalistic observation
4. Correlational
5. Independent
6. Treatment effect
7. Factorial
8. Valid
9. External
10. Generalized
11. Modus tollens

True/False: Self Test
1. True
2. True
3. False
4. True
5. True
6. False
7. True
8. False
9. True
10. True

Multiple Choice: Self Test
1. D
2. C
3. D
4. C
5. B
6. C
7. D
8. B
9. C
10. D
11. B
12. B
13. D
14. A
15. B

CHAPTER 3

Developing the Hypothesis

CHAPTER OBJECTIVES: CONCEPT CHECKS

The chapter objectives provide you with a concept checklist. These are things you should know after reading Chapter 3. The accompanying text page numbers are reference aids for your review.

1. Why do scientists consider their topics from ever changing perspectives? (53)

2. Testing our hypothesis about reality requires operational definitions. How does Chapter 3 define operational definitions and how are they applied when bonding our hypothesis to physical reality? (54)

3. How is construct validity important to our research procedures and measurements? (54)

4. Logically, what are the two fundamentally different types of hypotheses and what types of reasoning do they represent? (56-57)

5. Specify the steps involved in inductive and deductive reasoning. Give examples of their use. What are the limitations of these logical processes? (56-57)

6. Our goal in research is to use measurements that are both valid and reliable. Discuss the relationship between reliability and validity. How would you select methods of measurement that meet this goal? (58-60)

7. Describe the steps of the research process in terms of the decisions you are required to make at each step. (61)

8. Discuss several ways to find ideas for research. Relate this to your own system of searching for ideas. (61-70)

9. Wallas (1920) described the scientific process in four stages. Explain each in detail and formulate examples. (71-72)

10. What is the importance of library research in the scientific process? (72-74)

11. What tools are available in helping you to locate scientific information? Describe their different functions and the benefits of these methods of information gathering. (72-74)

12. Explain the concept of strong inference. Describe the four steps outlined by Platt (1964) and how this idea relates to psychology. (58)

STUDY GUIDE AND REVIEW

Key Terms

Define each of these terms in your own words. Check your understanding of Chapter 3 by referring to the featured text page.

1. Operational definitions (54)

2. Construct validity (54)

3. Inductive reasoning (56)

4. Deductive reasoning (57)

5. Strong inference (58)

6. Measurement (59)

7. Reliability (59)

8. Validity (59)

9. Preparation (71)

10. Incubation (72)

11. Illumination (72)

12. Verification (72)

13. Books in Print (73)

14. Journals (73)

15. Psychological Abstracts (74)

16. Computer Databases (74)

17. The Internet (75)

Fill-in: Self-Test

Fill in the missing word or phrase. Focus your attention on important Chapter 3 details.

1. Science is _____ in that it is based on observable phenomena and its conclusions can be checked by anyone. (54)

2. _____ define or represent our private ideas in terms of specific behaviors or concrete activities that anyone can witness or repeat. (54)

3. _____ asks whether the procedure that we are using is actually an adequate definition of the construct we are measuring. (55)

4. The process of generalizing from a specific incident to a more general idea is called _____ reasoning. (56)

5. Platt sees _____ not only as a method for rapid progress in science but also at the heart of every scientist's thinking. (58)

6. If reliability refers to consistency of a measuring instrument, then validity refers to _____. (59)

7. The _____ tells us briefly what information is covered in the journal article. (73)

8. Einstein demonstrated how ideas could be spontaneous and come from _____. (71)

9. According to Wallas (1920), having an interest in a problem and learning through library research describes _____. (71)

10. An operational definition defines events in terms of operations required to _____ them. This gives our idea a concrete meaning in reality. (54)

11. The stronger our research design, the better we are able to infer a(n) _____ between events. (57

12. _____, according to Wallas (1920), is testing an idea to see whether it fits the real world. (72)

True/False: Self Test

Test your understanding of Chapter 3 by marking the best answer to these true or false items.

1. _____ One problem with operational definitions is that a given concept may be defined in several possible ways. (54)

2. _____ General statements that address global questions are in ideal testable form. (57)

3. _____ Technically speaking, validity means the measure is consistent. (59)

4. _____ Measurement considerations strongly underlie the way we develop operational definitions. (59)

5. _____ A measurement can be reliable yet invalid. (59)

6. _____ It is important for individuals who make observations to be reliable in their ratings. (59)

7. _____ If your measures have been used previously, then it is unnecessary for you to determine the validity of your measures. (71)

8. _____ Wallas' first stage of the scientific process in which a scientist becomes interested and examines varied perspectives of the scientific problem is called verification. (71).

9. _____ Based on Wallas' description of problem-solving, new ideas infrequently appear spontaneously because incubation takes so many years. (72)

10. _____ The process of generalizing from a specific fact to a more general idea is called deduction. (56)

Multiple Choice: Self Test

Test your Chapter 3 comprehension by circling the best answer to these multiple choice questions.

1.   The process of generalizing from a specific instance to a more general idea is called _____ reasoning; on the other hand, the process of using a theory to predict a specific phenomenon is called _____ reasoning. (56-57)

    a. inductive, deductive
    b. deductive, inductive
    c. inferential, descriptive
    d. reliable, valid
    e. concrete, logical

2.   To make our hypotheses concrete we should redefine the concept of interest in terms of clearly observable operations that any one can see and repeat which requires _____. (54)

    a. operational definitions
    b. intuition
    c. revelation
    d. research
    e. statistics

3.   Wallas (1926) found that one of the things that scientists do to solve problems is to learn all they can about a problem and to examine it from varied perspectives. This stage of science is called _____. (71-72)

    a. preparation
    b. incubation
    c. illumination
    d. verification
    e. induction

·4. _____ refers to the consistency of an instrument used to measure a phenomenon. _____
refers to its accuracy in measuring a phenomenon. (59)

   a. validity, Reliability
   b. reliability, Validity
   c. internal validity, External validity
   d. external validity, Internal validity

5. What library resource would most likely be a primary source for experimental reports
written by scientists? (73-74)

   a. books
   b. popular science magazines
   c, journals
   d. the internet
   e. All of the above

6. According to Platt (1964), which of the following is a characteristic of strong inference?
(58)

   a. developing alternative hypotheses
   b. experimentation to exclude hypotheses
   c. careful experimentation to get clear results
   d. refining hypotheses
   e. All of the above

7. Which major index covers research related to psychology? (73-74)

   a. *Psychological Abstracts*
   b. InfoTrac
   c. *Social Science Citation Index*
   d. All of the above

8. What is a major advantage of the *Social Science Citation Index* (SSCI) over the other
indexes? (75)

   a. It includes a separate volume listing all studies that cited a particular study.
   b. It is possible to search a large body of bibliographic information in seconds.
   c. It is an online database system.
   d. All of the above

9.   A(n) _____ is a testable statement about the expected relationship between variables. (77-78)

   a. construct
   b. measurement
   c. hypothesis
   d. operational definition

10.   Which of the following is not a step required prior to experimentation? (60)

   a. Definition of independent and dependent variables
   b. Operational definitions of how the independent and dependent variables are to be measured, and consideration of the reliability and validity of each
   c. Statement of expected relationship between the variables
   d. Drafting an abstract written in past tense following APA guidelines that includes the expected outcome, number of subjects, procedures, statistical analysis, and conclusion

11.   The clock on the classroom wall is exactly one hour off. In terms of reliability and validity what would you conclude? (59)

   a. not reliable, not valid
   b. reliable, not valid
   c. not reliable, valid
   d. reliable, valid

12.   Platt likens the procedure of strong inference to climbing a tree, when each choice is _____ the previous one taken. (58)

   a. independent of
   b. unrelated to
   c. dependent on
   d. Both a and b

13.   Through what process would one predict observations from a well-established theory? (57)

   a. Induction
   b. Validation
   c. Deduction
   d. All of the above

14. The process of generalizing from a specific instance to a more general idea describes _____ reasoning. (56)

    a. intuitive
    b. inductive
    c. deductive
    d. Both a and c

15. The consistency of the research participants' response is determined by _____. (60)

    a. test-retest reliability
    b. true weight
    c. external validity
    d. all of the above

Essays

Apply your knowledge of Chapter 3 as you analyze the following questions in detail. Specifically refer to information in the chapter to support your answers.

1. What four things should you do to turn your research idea into a testable hypothesis?

2. Describe Platt's four steps illustrating strong inference and discuss why this process is advantageous for science.

3. Why aren't operational definitions necessarily the same for specific variables in different research studies?

4. Logically there are two fundamentally different types of hypotheses. Discuss the different questions asked by each and identify the type of reasoning utilized.

5. Describe ways that measurement can be reliable yet invalid.

RESEARCH ACTIVITIES

The goal of the research activities are to: (1) relate Chapter 3 on an applied learning dimension, and (2) get you involved in research.

1. **Mapping Out Research Ideas.** Give yourself permission to freely express any ideas that come to mind without any restrictions. Place your pen on the paper and do not lift it until the instructor notifies you to do so after 5 minutes. Begin in the middle of a blank piece of paper with the first thought that comes to mind. Continue by mapping all ideas that come to mind. Your goal is to use your creativity and fill every bit of white space that you can on your paper. After your instructor calls time, go back and group your ideas into general areas. Finally, rank your ideas in order of interest. Turn this paper in to your instructor and arrange for individual time to discuss possible research ideas.

2. **Daily Journal of Research Ideas.** Keep a daily journal of research ideas or questions that come to mind. Your goal is one idea per day. This exercise should become a habit for those who wish to become serious researchers. You will be amazed at the timing of some of your most inspirational ideas. Format your ideas into research questions and hypotheses. Don't hesitate to use the library in search of ideas and supporting information. For each idea check the library to determine whether information in this area is: (a) abundant, (b) scattered, but with a lot of related/supporting information, or (c) scarce. Turn this in to your instructor.

3. **Gaining Library Skills.** Use InfoTrac to research articles related to psychology.

    Assignment: Conduct a **literature search** on <u>one</u> of the following topics:

    * Effectiveness of mentoring at-risk youth
    * Utilization of mental health services among Latinos
    * Benefits of volunteerism
    * Improving proenvironmental behaviors

    A. **Find the key words.** Use the Thesaurus of Psychological terms or the Online InfoTracThesaurus to identify the key words to use in your search.
    B. **Refine your search.** Combine your key words with **AND, OR, NOT,** and report the number of records displayed for each search. Print out this exercise and turn it in to your instructor.
    C. **Identify information in the abstracts.** Select and read two abstracts. Record the following information: Author, title of the article, journal (year, volume and pages), hypotheses, and a brief summary of the results.

4. **Depression Among College Students. Developing Hypotheses.** Go to the library and use one of the many resources available (scientific journal articles, Info Trac, PsycInfo, Psychological Abstracts, etc.) to locate four articles related to the topic of depression. Determine which types of measurement instruments were used to measure the construct of depression. Describe how the concept of depression is operationally defined in each study and how the multitude of definitions may confuse/clarify and refine the construct of depression. Finally, after conducting your review of the literature, formulate your own operational definition of depression as well as a testable research question related to student depression.

5. **Empirical Test of Clichés.** Describe in detail how you might empirically test these common sense sayings about behavior: Develop research questions for each and consider possible research designs.

   a. birds of a feather flock together
   b. absence makes the heart grow fonder
   c. it takes one to know one

6. **Finding Psychological Articles and Tests on the Internet.** Search the internet for information on psychological articles related to personality and social psychology. Also, search the internet for personality tests like the Myers-Briggs. Print one psychological article and one psychological test from your internet search.

7. **Biographies of Scientists.**
   Use InfoTrac to find a biography on a noted scientist in psychology (e.g., Wilhelm Wundt, B. F. Skinner, Sigmund Freud, Kurt Lewin, Leon Festinger, Fritz Heider, etc.).
   How does their life story interface with their contribution to psychology?

RESEARCH SUMMARY AND DISCUSSION QUESTIONS

Developing Hypotheses

Darley, J. M., & Latane, B. (1968). Bystander intervention in emergencies: Diffusion of responsibility. *Journal of Personality and Social Psychology, 8*, 377-383.

      This research exemplifies Ray's point in Chapter 3 that ideas come from everywhere. The idea for this research study came from a tragic incident that occurred in 1964. A young woman, Kitty Genovesee, was violently murdered outside her New York apartment while 38 witnesses watched from their apartment windows. No one called for help. This led social psychologists, like John Darley and Bibb Latane, to ask questions about when people help. Darley and Latane hypothesized that when many people witness an emergency, individuals reason that someone else will help; this is called diffusion of responsibility.

      Darley and Latane tested their hypotheses in a series of ingenious experiments. In this study, college students were randomly to experimental conditions to discuss their personal college adjustment with other students via an intercom. In group 1, students thought they were participating with only one other student. In group 2, students were told they were participating with two other students; and in group 3, students were told they were participating with five other students. In reality all participants were alone and talking to a confederate on the intercom who simulated having a seizure. The dependent variable was whether or not people sought help in this perceived emergency, and the independent variable was how many people students thought witnessed the emergency. It was found that students were more likely to seek help when they thought there was only witness, and they were less likely to help when they thought there were other witnesses.

Discussion Questions

1. Discuss how Darley and Latane made their hypotheses concrete.

2. Find other information on bystander intervention and diffusion of responsibility by Darley and Latane. Discuss whether or not the findings of this experiment are reliable.

SUGGESTED READINGS

Douglas, N.E., & Baum, N. (1984). *Library research guide to psychology: Illustrated research strategy and sources*. Ann Arbor; MI: Pierian Press.

Weaver, D. B. (1982). *How to do a literature search in psychology*. Dallas, Texas: Resource Press.

Great reference guides for the beginning researcher.

ANSWERS

Fill-in: Self Test
1. Objective
2. Operational definitions
3. Construct validity
4. Inductive
5. Strong Inference
6. Accuracy
7. Abstract
8. Intuition
9. Preparation
10. Measure
11. Relationship
12. Verification

True/False: Self Test
1. True
2. False
3. False
4. True
5. True
6. True
7. False
8. False
9. False
10. False

Multiple Choice: Self Test

1. A
2. A
3. A
4. B
5. C
6. E
7. D
8. A
9. C
10. D
11. B
12. C
13. C
14. B
15. A

CHAPTER 4

Description of Behavior Through Numerical Representation

CHAPTER OBJECTIVES: CONCEPT CHECKS

The chapter objectives provide you with a concept checklist. These are things you should know after reading Chapter 4. The accompanying text page numbers are reference aids for your review.

1. Measurement theory requires us to ask what two questions when doing research? (85)

2. Compare and contrast the different scales of measurement. (86-88)

3. Cite two ways to display data. (90-91)

4. What three measures of central tendency are discussed in the text, and what are their characteristics? (93-95)

5. Discuss the concept of variability. Give examples of three different measures of variability and describe their functions. (95-99)

6. Why is it common to transform data? Relate transformation of data to the concept of z-scores. (102=103)

7. What is correlation? How does it aid us in understanding the relationship between variables? (105)

8. How would you define a positive correlation? How would you define a negative correlation? (107)

9. What can you say about the effect of one variable on the other in correlational studies? (107)

10. What information is derived from squaring the correlation coefficient? How does this relate to variability accounted for? (107-109)

11. Why is it important to assess underlying distribution before calculating correlations? (109)

STUDY GUIDE AND REVIEW

Key Terms

Define each of these terms in your own words. Check your understanding of Chapter 4 by referring to the featured text page.

1. Measurement (85)

2. Scales of measurement (86-88)

3. Nominal (86)

4. Ordinal (87)

5. Interval (88)

6. Ratio (88)

7. Qualitative (87)

8. Quantitative (87)

9. Equal intervals (88)

10. Frequency distribution (90)

11. Ordinate (91)

12. Abscissa (91)

13. Bar graph (91)

14. Frequency polygon (91)

15. Normal distribution (91)

16. Bimodal distribution (91)

17. Positively skewed distribution (93)

18. Negatively skewed distribution (93)

19. Measures of central tendency (93-95)

20 Mean (93)

21. Median (93)

22. Mode (94)

23. Measures of variability (95)

24. True score (95)

25. Dispersion (95)

26. Range (95)

27. Variance (95-97)

28. Sum of squares (97)

29. Deviation method (97)

30. Computational method (97)

31. Standard deviation (100)

32. Line graph (101)

33. Bar graph (101)

34. Linear transformation (102)

35. Meaningfulness (102)

36. z-scores (103)

37. Standard score (03)

38. Measure of association (104-106)

39. Scatterplot (104)

40 Correlation (104

41. Positive correlation (104)

42. Negative correlation (104)

43. Partitioned variance (109)

44. Curvilinear distribution (110)

Fill-in: Self Test

Fill in the missing word or phrase. Focus your attention on important Chapter 4 details.

1. In experimental studies behaviors are usually expressed in _____ terms. (85)

2. Frequency of response, intensity of response, duration of response, and reaction time are all examples of appropriate _____. (85)

3. _____ is a simple way to describe the relationship between variables. (85)

4. How we measure things is part of the field of study referred to as _____. It requires one to question what we can measure in research and what the measurements mean. (85)

5. A number may convey different types of information depending upon how it is used. Assigning numbers in terms of their identity, magnitude, equal intervals, and absolute zero defines _____. (86-87)

6. Another name for a nominal scale of measurement is _____. (86)

7. The difference between nominal categories is more _____ than quantitative. (87)

8. Ordinal scales can be obtained whenever you _____ subjects or events along a single dimension. (87)

9. The vertical (Y) axis on a graph is called the _____. (91)

10. In graphing, the horizontal (X) axis is called the _____. (91)

11. We call a distribution _____ if it approximates a bell-shaped distribution. (91)

12. The measure of central tendency that represents the most frequently occurring score is the _____. (94)

13. The _____ is the middle score that has an equal number of scores both above and below it. (93)

14. In a(n) _____ distribution, the mean is affected by extreme scores. (95)

15. Correlation does not help us to establish _____ between two variables since there may be effects due to a third unknown variable. (106)

True/False: Self Test

Test your understanding of Chapter 4 by marking the best answer to these true or false items.

1. _____ Understanding basic statistical properties is important in determining the appropriateness of a measure. (85)

2. _____ Computers are no replacement for understanding the fundamentals of statistical processes, graphing, and analysis. (85)

3. _____ Numbers can be used to represent many things. However, one must be careful not to use numbers themselves to name categories. (86-87)

4. _____ The ordinal scale represents some degree of quantitative difference whereas the nominal scale does not. (87)

5. _____ With ordinal scales you are making statements about order and the equal differences between values. (87)

6. _____ The most common ratio scales are found in the measurement of physical attributes of objects. (88)

7. _____ In the interval scale of measurement there is an absolute zero. (88)

8. _____ Variance does not describe the amount of variability in the same unit of measurement as the original data. (95)

9. _____ Variance is the square root of the standard deviation. (97)

10. _____ Z-scores can be either positive or negative. (103)

Multiple Choice: Self Test

Test your Chapter 4 comprehension by circling the best answer to these multiple choice questions.

1. Which of the following is an example of a statistical descriptor? (93)

    a. mode
    b. mean
    c. variance
    d. standard deviation
    e. All of the above

2. You have a study partner who says she has an IQ of 130. Given that the mean IQ is 100 and the standard deviation is 15, what would you conclude about your study partner's intelligence? (109)

    a. she's above the average in intelligence
    b. her intelligence is 2 standard deviation units above the average
    c. her intelligence z score is +2.00
    d. All of the above

3. In science numbers are used to _____. (86)

    a. Categorize
    b. Rank
    c. Quantify
    d. All of the above

4. Diagnosing someone as either schizophrenic, paranoid or neurotic is one example of what scale of measurement? (86-87)

   a. Nominal
   b. Ordinal
   c. Interval
   d. Ratio

5. Classifying patients as highly anxious, moderately anxious, or not at all anxious would be an example of using a(n) _____ scale of measurement. (87)

   a. nominal
   b. ordinal
   c. interval
   d. ratio

6. The number of correct answers on a statistics test represents a(n) _____ scale of measure. (88)

   a. nominal
   b. ordinal
   c. interval
   d. ratio

7. The distribution of intelligence scores among a large sample of graduate students at a top university were: mode= 130, median= 120, and mean= 110.
What would you conclude about the shape of this distribution? (91)

    a. normal
    b. bimodal
    c. positively skewed
    d. negatively skewed
    e. None of the above

8. What statistical term can be used to describe "typical"? (93)

    a. Mean
    b. Median
    c. Mode
    d. All of the above

9. The statistical term obtained by adding all scores and then dividing by the number of scores is the _____. (93)

    a. median
    b. mean
    c. sum of squares
    d. standard deviation

10. To understand the degree of association between attitudes towards condoms and risky sexual behavior one should _____. (104-110)

    a. draw a graph
    b. transform scores to a ratio scale of measure
    c. convert all scores to a ratio scale of measure
    d. find the correlation
    e. All of the above

11. In a _____ distribution, the mode, median, and mean all have the same value. (91)

    a. bimodal
    b. positively skewed
    c. normal
    d. negatively skewed

12. Which of the following is <u>not</u> a common measure of dispersion? (97)

    a. Range
    b. Standard deviation
    c. z-scores
    d. Variance

13. Which measure of variability is best known for its easy computation? (97)

    a. Range
    b. Sum of squares
    c. Variance
    d. Mode

14. The average of squared deviations from the mean is the _____. (97-98)

    a. standard deviation
    b. sum of squares
    c. variance
    d. z-score

15. To understand the degree of association between attitudes towards condoms and risky sexual behavior one should _____. (104-110)

    a. find the correlation
    b. conduct an analysis of variance
    c. conduct a path analysis
    d. conduct a multiple regression
    e. All of the above

16. If we found that the correlation between alcohol use in high school and GPA was r= -.75, you would conclude that _____. (104-110)

    a. alcohol causes poor grades
    b. alcohol use is unrelated to grades
    c. alcohol use in high school is negatively related to getting good grades
    d. alcohol use in high school is related to improved grades

17. If we found that the correlation between alcohol use in high school and GPA was r= -.75, how much would you say alcohol consumption accounted for grades? (107)

    a. -.75
    b. 75%
    c. .87
    d. 56%
    e. can not determine

18. The appropriate graph for a correlation is a _____. (104)

    a. frequency polygon
    b. line graph
    c. bar graph
    d. scatter diagram

Essays

Apply your knowledge of Chapter 4 as you analyze the following questions in detail. Specifically refer to information in the chapter to support your answers.

1. List the specific properties of each scale of measurement. Cite examples of each.

2. You plan to enter a highly competitive doctoral program in psychology. To improve your scores on the GRE you investigate three GRE preparation programs. Program 1 reported a mean improvement of 100 points. Program 2 reported a median improvement of 100 points. Program 3 reported a mode improvement of 100 points. Which program seems to have the best record? Explain your reasoning related to measures of central tendency.

3. Explain the reason for describing data in terms of both of central tendency and variability. Is it possible to have two distributions of the same size with identical mean averages that have different variabilities among scores? Explain and refer to examples.

4. What is correlation? Define its characteristics and application to research. What conclusions are inappropriate and why must you be cautious?

5. Discuss the use of the correlation coefficient for obtaining information regarding the amount of variability in one measure accounted for by another measure?

6. Define skewed distribution. Refer to measures of central tendency in describing skew. Why is the mean the measure of central tendency that is the most influenced by extreme scores? Draw a positively and negatively skewed distribution. Note the position of the mean, median, and mode on each distribution.

7. Discuss the use of graphs in descriptive statistics. Why is graphing a distribution an important first step? What are some important features of graphs?

8. Explain the reasoning for transformation of scores. What are the benefits? Define z-score. Relate transformation to z-scores to the concept of meaningfulness.

9. Identify the scale of measurement used in each of the following examples (i.e., nominal, ordinal, ratio, interval). What type of descriptive statistic would be appropriate for each?

   a. anxiety scale (1-7)
   b. cost of housing in Los Angeles
   c. final grades in research methods
   d. birth weights in Ethiopia
   e. deaths attributed to suicides in December
   f. income tax brackets
   g. religious denomination
   h. ranking preferences for beer
   i. ethnic distribution in San Francisco
   j. reported happiness scale (1-7)
   k money donated to charity
   l. divorce rates in California

RESEARCH ACTIVITIES

The goals of the research activities are to: (1) relate Chapter 4 on an applied learning dimension, and (2) get you involved in research.

1. **Physical Activity and Mood: A Correlational Study.**
   For one week record the information using the following scales:

   <u>Rate your level of physical activity on the following scale:</u>

   1. Very physically active
   2. Moderately physically active
   3. Somewhat physically active
   4. Not very physically active
   5. Very physically inactive

   <u>Rate your level of mood on the following scale:</u>

   1. Very good mood
   2. Relatively good mood
   3. Neutral
   4. Somewhat of a bad mood
   5. Very bad mood

Date	Time of day	Physical Activity Rating	Mood Rating
1.			
2.			
3.			
4.			
5.			
6.			
7.			

Research Flowchart: Fill in the following information.

A. State your research hypothesis.

B. Operationally define your variables.

C. State measures you controlled or held constant.

D. Graph data on a scatterplot. Label the axes and the graph.

E. Calculate by using the Pearson's correlation coefficient.

F. Interpret. State the coefficient of determination.

2. **Parents, Sex Information, and Risk Taking Behavior: A Correlational Study.**
   Administer the following survey to at least 15 individuals.

   This survey involves information regarding sexual attitudes and behavior. I will be using the information gathered from this survey to gain knowledge about graphing data. No names should be indicated on the survey, and all information will be kept completely confidential. If there are any questions that you do not wish to answer, please feel free to skip to the next question. Thank you for your participation.

   What is your gender? Male _____ Female _____

   For the following questions please circle your response: 1, 2, 3, 4 or 5.

   1. Did your parents discuss sex and its risks with you while you lived at home as an adolescent?

1   2   3   4   5

Not at all   Very much

2. How knowledgeable do you believe you are regarding sexually transmitted diseases, AIDS, and the risks of pregnancy?

1   2   3   4   5
Not at all   Very

3. How much do you feel the information which your parents shared about sex and its risks has influenced your willingness to engage in safe sexual behaviors (e.g., using condoms)?

1   2   3   4   5

No influence   Significant

a. State your research hypotheses.
b. Organize a scatterplot of the data obtained from questions 2 and 3 into a scatterplot. The abscissa should be labeled "Degree of Knowledge" (values 1-5). The ordinate should be labeled "Degree of Influence" (values 1-5).
c. Calculate a Pearson's Product Moment Correlation Coefficient between for the data obtained from questions 1 and 2, questions 1 and 3, and questions 2 and 3.
d. Interpret the results by explaining what type of relationships, if any, are supported by the data. Discuss inferences about causation.

3. **Assess Your Self Esteem.** Complete the following questions. Identify each item as either a nominal, ordinal, interval, or ratio number.

Social Security Number _____
Male (01) _____ Female (02) _____
Year of Birth _____
Age _____
Class Standing:
Freshman (1) _____ Sophomore (2) _____ Junior (3) _____ Senior (4) _____
Exact time you started this test? _____

Rosenberg Self Esteem Scale

This questionnaire asks questions about self esteem. Answer the following questions honestly using the response scale below. There are no right and wrong answers.

1   Strongly agree
2   Agree
3   Disagree
4   Strongly disagree

_____ 1.   I feel that I am a person of worth, at least on an equal basis with others.

_____ 2.   I feel that I have a number of good qualities.

_____ 3.   *All in all, I'm inclined to feel that I am a failure.

_____ 4.   I am able to do things as well as most other people.

_____ 5.   *I feel if I do not have much to be proud of.

_____ 6.   I take a positive attitude toward myself.

_____ 7.   On the whole, I am satisfied with myself.

_____ 8.   *I wish I could have more respect for myself.

_____ 9.   *I certainly feel useless at times.

_____10.   *At times I think I am no good at all.

        *Reverse score these items

4. **Misleading with the Average.**
   Entry level salary data was collected on small sample of college graduates who earned degrees in psychology and biology. Find the mean, median, and mode for each group. If you wanted to persuade someone that they should definitely pursue a degree in psychology, which measure of central tendency would you use? If you wanted to emphasize that it really didn't matter what they majored in, which measure of central tendency would you use?

   Entry Level Salaries for Graduates in:

Psychology	Biology
$30.000	$30,000
$36,000	$36,000
$40,000	$40,000
$42,000	$42,000
$149,000	$49,000

5. **Misleading with Statistics.**
   Use InfoTrac to find articles about how statistics can lie. Explain this effect. Also see the suggested reading list at the end of this chapter.

RESEARCH SUMMARY AND DISCUSSION QUESTIONS

Description of Behavior Through Numerical Representation

Holmes, T. H., & Rahne, R. H. (1967). The social adjustment rating scale. *Journal of Psychosomatic Research, 11,* 213-218.

This article demonstrates how psychological experiences, like life stress, can be described, measured and statistically summarized using numbers. In Chapter 5, Ray discussed different ways in which numbers are used. Holmes and Rahne developed the Social Readjustment Rating Scale (SRRS) to measure life stress and social readjustment associated with life events. They found that the death of a spouse was ranked as the most stressful life event, and that minor violations of the law were ranked the least stressful life event. Interestingly, even positive life events like marriage, pregnancy, and outstanding personal achievement were ranked as highly stressful. Subsequent research found that this scale has been useful in identifying chronic stress and predicting illness.

Discussion Questions

1. Explain how numbers were used on the Social Readjustment Rating Scale to establish the ratings of stressful life events and social readjustment. Explain your   answer in terms of scale of measurement.
2. What type of statistical analysis was used to assess the reliability of the SRRS?
3. To examine the relationship between stress and illness, what type of statistical analysis would be appropriate? Explain your answer.

SUGGESTED READINGS

Huff, D., & Geis, I. (1994). *How to lie with statistics.* New York: W. W. Norton.

This amusing book is easy reading full of actual examples of statistical misuses.

SOURCES

Bryant, R. (1974). Statistics for the simple. *Phi Beta Kappa School Research Information Service Quarterly, 7,* 3.

ANSWERS

Fill-in: Self Test
1. Quantitative
2. Measures
3. Correlation
4. Measurement theory
5. Scales of measurement
6. Categorical
7. Qualitative
8. Rank
9. Ordinate
10. Abscissa
11. Normal
12. Mode
13. Median
14. Skewed
15. Causality

<u>True/False: Self Test</u>

1. True
2. True
3. False
4. True
5. False
6. True
7. False
8. True
9. False
10. True

<u>Multiple Choice: Self Test</u>

1. E
2. D
3. D
4. A
5. B
6. D
7. D
8. D
9. B
10. B
11. C
12. C
13. A
14. C
15. A
16. C
17. D
18. D

CHAPTER 5

Inferential Statistics: Making Statistical Decisions

CHAPTER OBJECTIVES: CONCEPT CHECKS

The chapter objectives provide you with a concept checklist. These are things you should know after reading Chapter 5. The accompanying text page numbers are reference aids for your review.

1   How are inferential statistics used in research? (115)

2.   How are samples useful in understanding the characteristics of a given population? (115)

3.   How are probability statements used in statistical research results? What is meant by "chance alone"? (117)

4.   Relate the "gamblers' fallacy" to the idea of independent outcomes. (117)

5.   What is the rule for determining the probability of two independent events? (118)

6.   What is a normal distribution? Describe its characteristics. How does it provide us with a mathematical model that we can use to interpret statistical events? (120-123)

7.   How do you calculate and interpret the standard deviation? (124)

8.   What is the null hypothesis? What is meant by rejecting the null hypothesis? (125-126)

9.   What parameters are important to consider in statistical hypothesis testing? (127)

10. How can we use sample variance to estimate population variance? (127)

11. Degrees of freedom refer to what? (128)

STUDY GUIDE AND REVIEW

<u>Key Terms</u>

Define each of these terms in your own words. Check your understanding of Chapter 5 by referring to the featured text page.

1. Inferential statistics (115)

2. Population (115)

3. Sample (115)

4. Parameters (127)

5. Random sampling (115)

6. Probability (116)

7. Gamblers' fallacy (117)

8. Normal distribution (120-121)

9. Probability distribution (120-121)

10. Hypothesis testing (125)

11. Null hypothesis (125)

12. Reject the null hypothesis (125-126)

13. t-test for independent groups (126-130)

14. Analysis of variance (130)

15. Population parameters (127)

16. Sample statistics (127)

17. Degrees of freedom (128)

18. t-table (129)

19. One-tailed test (129)

20. Two-tailed test (129)

Fill-in: Self Test

Fill in the missing word or phrase. Focus your attention on important Chapter 5 details.

1.   A complete set of all possible samples is known as a(n) _____. (115)

2.   _____ are used to infer from a given sample the parameters related to the population. (115)

3.   _____ exists when each member of a population is equally likely to be chosen. (115)

4.   By "chance alone" means the results were not due to the experimental _____. (117)

5.   If you toss a coin five times and each time it results in heads up. You become confident that the probability is high that the next toss will result in tails up. This faulty thinking illustrates the _____. (117)

6.   If one event is not related to another, they are said to be _____. (117)

7.   Given any individual who is randomly chosen there is a(n) _____% chance that he or she will have an IQ score that is within one standard deviation of the population mean. (122)

8.   In hypothesis testing, the hypothesis that specifies that the population mean is the same as the sample mean is referred to as the _____. (125)

9.   If the null hypothesis cannot be _____, then we cannot claim that our subjects came from a different population. (125)

10. Statistically, the _____ examines the difference between two sets of ranks. (126)

11. If you are interested in statistical differences that are unidirectional you would conduct a _____ -tailed test. (129)

12. Hypothesis tests that examine general differences, regardless of direction, are referred to as _____. (129)

True/False: Self Test

Test your understanding of Chapter 5 by marking the best answer to these true or false items.

1. _____ Implicit in the technical language of inferential statistics is the assumption that the sample was drawn randomly or systematically. (115)

2. _____ The odds of tossing a coin so that it lands heads up is higher if all previous coin tosses have landed tails up. (117)

3. _____ The gamblers' fallacy assumes the outcome of one event is independent and not influenced by previous events. (117)

4. _____ Different symbols are used to express population mean and sample mean. (127)

5. _____ Hypothesis testing is one of the main branches of descriptive statistics. (125)

6. _____ t-tests can be used to evaluate the difference between the means of two experimental groups. (126-130)

7. _____ As time goes by in a coin toss, the odds of head turning up increases. (117)

8. _____ The majority of people have an IQ within one standard deviation of the mean IQ of 100. (122)

9. _____ The Central Limit Theorem is the heart of inferential statistics. (123)

10. _____ Confidence intervals define where you expect to find the sample mean to be found. (125)

Multiple Choice: Self Test

Test your Chapter 5 comprehension by circling the best answer to these multiple choice questions.

1. What is the probability of winning the coin toss at the beginning of a football game? (117)

    a. .05
    b. .01
    c. .5
    d. .1

2. A curve whose characteristics include 68.26% of all scores between the mean plus and minus one standard deviation is descriptive of _____ . (122)

    a. the normal distribution
    b. positive skew
    c. degrees of freedom
    d. a bimodal frequency polygon

3. Within two standard deviations of the mean fall _____% of all scores. (122)

    a. 2.28
    b. 13.59
    c. 95.44
    d. 99.74

4. To test if the ranks in one group are different from the ranks in another group, what statistical test would we strongly consider? (126-130)

    a. t-test for independent samples
    b. t-test for dependent samples
    c. Pearson's r
    d. Spearman's r

5. Which of the following is an example of a statistical test? (126-130)

    a. t-test for independent samples
    b. Pearson's r
    c. t-test for matched scores
    d. All of the above

6. What term refers to the number of scores that are free to vary? (128)

    a. Parameters
    b. Degrees of freedom
    c. N
    d. Variance

7. What is an important assumption in utilizing a t-test for independent groups? (129-130)

    a. A control group
    b. Random assignment of subjects
    c. Validity
    d. Large N

8. If the same twenty individuals were tested before and after a treatment, what inferential test would you likely apply? (130)

    a. Spearman's r
    b. t-test for independent groups
    c. t-test for matched groups
    d. Any of the above

9. According to the text, which of the following should be considered in statistical hypothesis testing? (126-130)

    a. Population variance
    b. Population mean
    c. Size of the sample
    d. All of the above

10. In the notation: $t(12)=3.98$, $p<.01$, what are the degrees of freedom? (128)

    a. 12
    b. 3.98
    c. .01
    d. Not enough information

11. The goal of inferential statistics is to _____. (115)

    a. describe distributions
    b. infer information from a sample to a population
    c. ask how sample statistics match the parameters of a population
    d. Both a and c

12. What does it mean if your results were significant at p< .001? (129)

   a. the probability of being correct is less than 1 in 1000
   b. the probability that our experimental manipulation worked is 1 in 1000
   c. the probability of finding these results by chance is less than 1 in 1000
   d. the probability of being right is more than 1 in 1000

13. A hypothesis that states that the larger the number of people in each sample the less variability is called the _____. (123)

   a. Central Limit Theorem
   b. inferential hypothesis
   c. null hypothesis
   d. alternative hypothesis

14. When you are comparing more than two groups you should employ (127)

   a. correlation
   b. t-test
   c. ANOVA
   d. population parameters

Essays

Apply your knowledge of Chapter 5 as you analyze the following questions in detail. Specifically refer to information in the chapter to support your answers.

1. Conceptually, if an experiment was run an infinite number of times, each time with a different sample of individuals from the population, this would represent all the possible outcomes of the experiment. Integrate this concept with probability theory and the normal distribution.

2. What is the central limit theorem? Explain how the size of the samples drawn from a population influences the variability of the means.

3. What are the characteristics of the normal distribution?

4. Identify the different symbols that we use for population parameters and sample statistics.

5. When might a t-test be used? What is the objective of the t-test?

6. Refer to Table 5.3 and write in words and in formal notation what can be inferred from this t-test.

7. Explain the difference between one-tailed and two-tailed tests. How do these different tests apply to the research prediction?

RESEARCH ACTIVITIES

The goals of the research activities are to: (1) relate Chapter 5 on an applied learning dimension, and (2) get you involved in research.

1. **Sports Psychology Research: Improving Athletic Performance with Mental Imagery.** As a sports psychologist, you are interested in the effects of mental imagery on swimming performance. Test if vivid mental imagery improves athletic performance. Design a two-group study to test this research question. Address the following:

    a. What are the null and alternative hypotheses?
    b. What is the independent variable?
    c. What is the dependent variable?
    d. What scale of measurement is your dependent variable?
    e. What type of statistic will you use?
    f. Where will you get your sample?
    g. How will subjects be assigned to groups?

2. **Sex-typing of Infants Research:** *Analysis Using t-test for Independent Samples*. Design a study to investigate sex-typing, which research shows begins at birth. Select twenty subjects to participate in your study. Randomly assign ten subjects to each group. Group 1 will rate a picture of a baby with a female name, Serena. Group 2 will rate a picture of a baby with a male name, Stephen. Ask your subjects to rate the baby on the given adjectives with respect to the accompanying rating scales. Collect your data. To score the responses, simply total the chosen values corresponding to each item. A high cumulative total would indicate a very positive rating of the baby on the given characteristics. A low cumulative total would indicate a very negative rating of the baby on the given characteristics.

We are student investigators in a college level experimental psychology course. We are learning how to design and perform experiments. As an assignment we are investigating nonverbal cues. Please rate this baby on the following characteristics, using your best intuition in making your decision. We are most interested in your first impression. Thank you for your participation.

[INSERT YOUR BABY PICTURE HERE]

Description:

Date of Birth: August 25
Place of Birth: Sacramento, California
Age: 6 months old
Gender: Female
Name: Serena

QUESTION: *In your own words, how would you describe this baby to your friends or relatives?*

Descriptive Comments.

RATING SCALES

(1) Strongly disagree
(2) Disagree
(3) Neutral
(4) Agree
(5) Strongly agree

1.	Healthy	1	2	3	4	5
2.	Strong	1	2	3	4	5
3.	Coordinated	1	2	3	4	5
4.	Active	1	2	3	4	5
5.	Intelligent	1	2	3	4	5
6.	Independent	1	2	3	4	5
7.	Good	1	2	3	4	5
8.	Attractive	1	2	3	4	5
9.	Outgoing	1	2	3	4	5
10.	Friendly	1	2	3	4	5
11.	Attentive	1	2	3	4	5
12.	Advanced	1	2	3	4	5

We are student investigators in a college level experimental psychology course. We are learning how to design and perform experiments. As an assignment we are investigating nonverbal cues. Please rate this baby on the following characteristics, using your best intuition in making your decision. We are most interested in your first impression. Thank you for your participation.

[Insert Your Baby Picture Here]

Description:

Date of Birth: August 25
Place of Birth: Sacramento, California
Age: 6 months old
Gender: Male
Name: Stephen

QUESTION: *In your own words, how would you describe this baby to your friends or relatives?*

Descriptive Comments.

RATING SCALES

(1) Strongly disagree
(2) Disagree
(3) Neutral
(4) Agree
(5) Strongly agree

1. Healthy   1   2   3   4   5

2. Strong   1   2   3   4   5

3. Coordinated   1   2   3   4   5

4. Active   1   2   3   4   5

5. Intelligent   1   2   3   4   5

6. Independent   1   2   3   4   5

7. Good   1   2   3   4   5

8. Attractive   1   2   3   4   5

9. Outgoing   1   2   3   4   5

10. Friendly   1   2   3   4   5

11. Attentive   1   2   3   4   5

12. Advanced   1   2   3   4   5

A. **Design a Step by Step Flow Chart Comparing Two Independent Groups.** Using the sex stereotyping research question, design a flowchart which describes the research design comparing two independent groups in a step by step process.

   Address the following issues: (a) sample selection, (b) assignment into groups, (c) manipulated variable, (d) control, (e) statistical tests, (f) conclusion, (f) possible limitations or threats to internal validity.

B. **Write a Research Abstract.** Based on the sex stereotyping study you conducted, write an abstract. State your research questions. How many subjects were used in your study? How did you acquire your sample? How would you describe your sample based on gender, age, educational status, and ethnicity? Identify the independent and dependent variables. Discuss the details of the procedure. Analyze the data using t-tests for independent groups. Show your work in your workbook. Report your t-test results. Did you reject the null hypothesis? What are your conclusions? What possible confounds may threaten the study's internal validity? Be prepared to discuss your research in class.

3. **Mozart and Baby IQ. Identify Threats to Validity.** In your work book analyze the following research scenario. Identify and discuss (a) the research hypothesis, (b) the independent and dependent variables, (c) threats to internal validity, and (d) other limitations.

   Investigators wanted to see if early exposure to an intellectually stimulating environment would produce a child that was higher in IQ. Couples with newborns were asked to volunteer. The age of newborn participants was between 0 and 6 weeks. All parents were required to be college graduates. Twenty-four couples volunteered to participate with their newborns for one year. The parents and their newborns were assigned to conditions based on their preference.

   Condition 1 required that Mozart be played around the clock in the baby's presence (including sleeping states). Noise levels were held constant. Further, the baby would be drilled with flash cards every day. Twelve babies and their parents participated in this condition.

   Condition 2 required that the baby have no exposure to Mozart and was not to be exposed to flash card drills. Twelve babies and their parents participated in this condition.

   At the end of the year the IQ of all participating children was assessed by a licensed child psychologist.

   a. Research Hypothesis:
   b. Independent and Dependent Variables:
   c. Threats to Internal Validity:
   d. Other Limitations:

4. **Cutting Edge Statistical Tests.** Use InfoTrac to find out what a meta-analysis is. Explain how this technique differs from the statistical tests mentioned in your text. See Zelezny (1998) on the suggested reading list at the end of this chapter for a clear example of a meta-analysis.

RESEARCH SUMMARY AND DISCUSSION QUESTIONS

Inferential Statistics: Making Statistical Decisions

Langer, E. J., & Rodin, J. (1976). The effects of choice and enhanced personal responsibility for the aged: A field experiment in an institutional setting. *Journal of Personality and Social Psychology, 34*, 191-198.

To find a significant difference between two groups Ray, in Chapter 5, described the usefulness of t-tests. This article by Langer and Rodin demonstrates the application of t-tests to determine the effect of choice on life satisfaction among elderly nursing home residents.

In this field experiment, residents in the responsibility treatment group were told that they had choices about their care and how to spend their time. In comparison, residents in the control group were not told they had choices; instead, they were told that the nursing home would make their lives comfortable and happy. Thus, the amount of control given to the residents was manipulated as the independent variable. Using t-tests it was found that residents that were given more choice and control fared better on all dependent variables that measured life satisfaction, activity, and alertness.

Discussion Questions
1. Are the hypotheses for this study one-tailed or two-tailed? Explain your answer.
2. If a significant difference was found between the responsibility treatment group and the comparison group, was the null hypothesis retained or rejected? Explain your answer with respect to hypothesis testing.
3. What is the probability that these results occurred by chance?

SUGGESTED READINGS

Rubin, J. Z., Provenzano, F. J., & Luria, Z. (1974). The eye of the beholder: Parents, views on sex of newborns. *American Journal of Orthopsychiatry, 44*, 512-519.

This study suggests that sex-typing and sex-role socialization begins at birth.

Zelezny, L. C. (1999). Effectiveness of environmental interventions to improve proenvironmental behavior: A meta-analysis. *Journal of Environmental Education, 32*, 5-14.

ANSWERS

Fill-in: Self Test
1. Population
2. Inferential statistics
3. Random sampling
4. Manipulation
5. Gamblers' fallacy
6. Independent
7. 68.26
8. Null hypothesis
9. Rejected
10. Wilcoxon Rank Test
11. One
12. Two-tailed

True/False: Self Test
1. True
2. False
3. False
4. True
5. False
6. True
7. False
8. True
9. True
10. False

Multiple Choice: Self Test
1. C
2. A
3. C
4. C
5. D
6. B
7. B
8. C
9. D
10. A
11. D
12. C
13. A
14. C

CHAPTER 6

Testing the Hypothesis: A Conceptual Introduction

CHAPTER OBJECTIVES: CONCEPT CHECKS

The chapter objectives provide you with a concept checklist. These are things you should know after reading Chapter 6. The accompanying text page numbers are reference aids for your review.

1. Evaluation of a research hypothesis is a complex process. Identify three important questions you should consider in your evaluation. (135)

2. What three resources do we use when looking for unknown factors that may be responsible for the experimental outcome? (135)

3. Why is chance always involved in our sampling and observations of the world? (135)

4. Why do we never state that the independent variable absolutely caused the effect on the dependent variable? (135)

5. Why is it essential that the initial phase of any experiment be a statistical decision process? (135)

6. What is the role of confounds in the research process? (135-136)

7. Why do we try to eliminate sources of uncontrolled variance that operate in a systematic manner? (136)

8. Why do scientists argue that the heart of experimentation lies in ruling out alternative explanations? (136)

9. What is the F-ratio? How can it be explained in terms of within-group variance and between-group variance? How does this relate to the treatment effect and error variance? (139)

10. What is the relationship between a calculated F-value that is close to 1 and the null hypothesis? What is the general rule regarding the value of the F-ratio and the certainty of differences between groups that are not caused by chance alone? (140)

11. What does it mean to assign a probability to a statement of our findings? (135)

12. What special name do we give our mistakes when rejecting and failing to reject the null hypothesis? Define these errors. (143)

13. What is the essence of power in experimentation? (143)

14. What is effect size and how is it related to Type II errors? (143)

15. Explain the conditions that improve the likelihood of obtaining positive experimental results. (137)

16. What are the three ways that variability can be described in experimentation? (138-141)

17. Describe the confounds that severely threaten internal validity. How can they be controlled? (149-149)

STUDY GUIDE AND REVIEW

Key Terms
Chapter 6 by referring to the featured text page.

1. Research hypothesis (135)

2. Null hypothesis (135)

3. Statistical decision process (135)

4. Confound hypothesis (136)

5. Uncontrolled variance operating in a systematic manner (136)

6. Control of factors that could influence a study (136)

7. Systematic (139-141)

8. Systematic variation (138)

9. Chance variation (138)

10. Nonsystematic variation (138-139)

11. Confound (136)

12. F-ratio (139)

13. Within-groups variance (139-140)

14. Between-groups variance (139-140)

15. Type I error (146)

16. Type II error (143)

17. Alpha level (143)

18. Beta level (143)

19. Power (143)

20. Effect size (143)

21. Error variation (138)

22. Secondary variance (140)

23. Threats to internal validity (145-149)

    a.   History (146)

    b.   Maturation (146-147)

    c.   Testing (147)

    d.   Instrumentation (147)

    e.   Statistical regression (147-148)

    f.   Selection (148)

    g.   Mortality (148)

    h.   Selection-Maturation interaction (148)

    i.   Diffusion (149)

24. Self-correcting nature of science (150)

Fill-in: Self Test

Fill in the missing word or phrase. Focus your attention on important Chapter 6 details.

1. Threats to _____ result from factors other than manipulation of the independent variable that could influence the research findings. (1245)

2. Experimental results may have occurred because of _____ and not because of a particular factor. (136)

3. The possibility that there are no differences between groups makes us consider the _____ hypothesis. (136)

4. Results may be due to _____, which are unspecified factors that severely threaten internal validity. (139)

5. To eliminate sources of uncontrolled variance that operate in a systematic manner, it is necessary to _____ factors that we know influence our results in a systematic way. (140-141)

6. Another name for uncontrolled systematic variance is _____, because it results from variables other than our independent variable. (140)

7. Chance variation may also be called _____ variation. (138)

8. In terms of the dependent variable, the difference between the experimental and control group is called the _____. (132)

9. When we incorrectly fail to reject the null hypothesis we have committed a _____. (143)

10. Subjects in one group may differ initially from the subjects in another group. This confound is called _____. (140)

11. An important initial step in the process of experimentation is to develop the research _____. (135)

12. According to the text, the cycle of scientific experimentation would best be described as a spiral that adds new information with each rotation. This is the underlying concept of the _____ nature of science. (150)

13. Subjects in an experiment may communicate with each other which may result in reducing the differences between the groups. This threat to internal validity is called _____. (149)

14. Cohen's d is a common measure of ____. (143)

15. Eta squared is the amount of variance associated with a ___ effect. (144)

True/False: Self Test

Test your understanding of Chapter 6 by marking the best answer to these true or false items.

1. _____ Chance is always involved in our sampling and observations of the world. (135)

2. _____ The null hypothesis is always one possible interpretation, even if there are striking differences between groups. (135)

3. _____ Logically, in research, if we establish that it was not chance that caused our results, then they must be due to the independent variable. (135)

4. _____ Confounds severely threaten internal validity but do not affect our interpretation of the results. (136)

5. _____ It is necessary to completely control every possible factor in our study. (136)

6. _____ Systematic variations refer to those factors that influence a group of subjects as a whole. (138)

7. _____ Almost anything can be a confound. (136)

8. _____ When we fail to reject the null hypothesis when it is actually false, we are committing a Type I error. (143)

9. _____ The goal of power calculations is to estimate the number of subjects we need depending upon the magnitude of change that our independent variable has on our dependent variable, thus reducing Type II errors. (143)

10. _____ A goal in designing experiments is to select an independent variable with a strong effect to reduce the chance of Type II errors. (143=144)

Multiple Choice: Self Test

Test your Chapter 6 comprehension by circling the best answer to these multiple choice questions.

1. Which of the following is an important determinant of the experimental design? (135)

    a. Internal validity
    b. Statistical analysis
    c. External validity
    d. All of the above

2. External validity is concerned with the _____ of research findings. (135)

    a. accuracy
    b. generalizability
    c. confounds
    d. error

3. In the process of experimentation, we have a set goal of understanding what part of our results are attributed to _____. (136)

    a. the effect of the IV on the DV
    b. chance
    c. confounds
    d. All of the above

4. In every experiment there are individual differences between participants. This variation is _____. (139)

    a. systematic
    b. unsystematic
    c. error
    d. a confound
    e. both b and c

5. Factors such as mental alertness, physical health, and emotional states are examples of factors that affect _____ variance. (139)

    a. between-group
    b. within-group
    c. explained
    d. systematic

6. When the IV has no effect, then the F-ratio is equal to approximately _____.
   (141)

   a. 0
   b. 1
   c. alpha
   d. r squared

7. If the ratio of between-groups variance to within-groups variance is close to 1.00,
   then _____. (141)

   a. we are able to reject the null hypothesis
   b. we are not able to reject the null hypothesis
   c. we have established statistical significance
   d. we have committed a Type I error

8. If $p < .01$, then _____. (144)

   a. results from our study could have happened by chance alone 1 out of 100 times
   b. the F-ratio is small and the results are not statistically significant
   c. results from the study could be due to manipulation of the IV in 1 out of 100
      times
   d. we have made an alpha error

9. When we reject the null hypothesis and claim we found a difference between groups
   when in fact the difference was the result of chance, we have committed a
   _____. (143)

   a. Type I error
   b. Type II error
   c. Beta error
   d. 1-Beta error

10. The probability that a researcher will make a Type I error is called
    _____. (143)

    a. alpha
    b. beta
    c. power
    d. F

11. A large F can be produced by _____. (144)

    a. increasing the between-group variance
    b. reducing the within-group variance
    c. decreasing power
    d. both a and b

12. _____ describes the tendency of extreme scores to regress towards the mean. (147)

    a. Selection
    b. Correlation
    c. Statistical regression
    d. Interaction

13. When subjects drop out, refuse to participate, or die, this is known as _____. (148)

    a. selection-maturation interaction
    b. mortality
    c. regression
    d. selection

14. When subjects in an experiment communicate with each other, this communication can reduce the difference between groups. This is called _____. (149)

    a. interaction
    b. diffusion
    c. dissension
    d. regression

15. If you rejected the null hypothesis and found a difference between the experimental and control group, how would you interpret this? (138-139)

    a. the independent variable was effective
    b. the independent variable may have been effective or we may have found the outcome by chance
    c. the difference may be due to an unexplained systematic confound variable
    d. both b and c

16. Systematic variation in an experiment may be due to _____. (139-140)

    a. the independent variable
    b. confounds
    c. error
    d. both a and b

17. Statistically the ratio between between-group variance and within-group variance is known as _____. (139)

    a. t
    b. F
    c. r
    d. R

Essays

Apply your knowledge of Chapter 6 as you analyze the following questions in detail. Specifically refer to information in the chapter to support your answers.

1. What does it mean to state that within-groups variance is high or low? Assume you have conducted an experiment using two groups. How is a researcher's decision, that the difference between the two groups is due to chance fluctuations in the performance of individuals influenced by the following: (1) size of the treatment effect and (2) variability of scores within groups?

2. When is the F-ratio used? Explain the F-ratio in terms of treatment effects and chance variance. What does it mean to find a calculated value of F= approximately 1? Relate calculated F-values to the null hypothesis. How can you improve your chances of finding significant differences between groups?

3. Design your own table to explain Type I and Type II errors. Use an example throughout to illustrate each cell and discuss the role of chance. What is a good way to distinguish between Type I and Type II errors? What can you do to prevent making a Type I or Type II error?

4. Describe in detail the three ways variability can be partitioned in an experiment. How do you identify and assess the presence of each? How do they affect your experimental conclusions?

5. Discuss Campbell and Stanley's threats to internal validity. Describe the possible confounds and their potential effect on the experiment. For each, discuss how you might control for the effects.

6. In a study conducted over a two year period on students' interest in school recycling, Zelezny (1998) found that prior to the implementation of district-wide school recycling students reported a very strong interest in participation; however, one year after the initiation of school recycling students reported less interest in participation. Are proenvironmental programs like school recycling detrimental to students' environmental interest? How would you interpret these findings? What threats to validity should be considered?

7. Comment on the text's circular description of the experimental process. Do you agree or disagree with this representation? How might this schema be improved?

RESEARCH ACTIVITIES

The goals of the research activities are to: (1) relate Chapter 6 on an applied learning dimension, and (2) get you involved in research.

1. **TV Violence and Aggression: Develop a Research Hypothesis and Outline an Introduction.** Develop a research hypothesis relating exposure to TV violence and aggression. Clearly identify the variables, the population, and the predicted outcome or relationship between variables. Locate five current supporting research articles related to your topic. Outline an introduction and turn this in to your instructor for feedback. See Chapter 15 of your text for guidance. Alphabetize your references and develop an APA style reference page.

2. **Identify the Confounds and Threats to Internal Validity.** For the following four studies (A, B, C, and D) identify the independent and dependent variables. Identify and discuss the threats to internal validity. How would you improve these studies?

   (A) Researchers want to test whether **mountain climbing will increase strength, perceived competence, and immune system functioning** in juvenile delinquents. A one-week mountain climbing expedition to Mount Whitney is planned. Twenty-five male adolescents in a Los Angeles County rehabilitation facility have volunteered for the project. Twenty-five male adolescents from a San Diego County rehabilitation facility will be randomly selected to serve as a control group. The project will begin August 8 and end August 15. All subjects will be tested daily at 5 p.m. on: (1) strength as measured using a dynamometer which is a valid measure of grip strength, (2) perceived competence as measured by a questionnaire, and (3) immune system functioning as measured by the volume of t-cells in blood samples.

   (B) The infamous sleep researcher, R. U. Asleep, wanted to study the **effects of REM (Rapid Eye Movement) sleep deprivation on maze running ability**. The experimental group consisted of five male hamsters all from the same litter to control for age, gender and genetics. The control group consisted of five male hamsters from another litter. Baseline maze-running ability was established for both experimental and control groups. The experimenter set up small individual running wheels, which were fully enclosed to control for hamster location. Hamsters in the experimental group slept inside the wheels to adapt to the apparatus. The experimental group was deprived of REM sleep for 120 hours in the following manner. REM sleep was detected by using electromyography. At the onset of REM in the experimental condition the running wheel would begin to turn in a clockwise motion and force the hamster to wake up and run. Maze-running ability was tested every twenty-four hours for all subjects.

(C) The local school district wants to **compare three anti-smoking programs used at the sixth grade level.** The superintendent makes the following assignments based upon his own best judgment. School 1 will view a film program that features prominent celebrities promoting the anti-smoking message. School 2 will listen to guest lecturers who are suffering from lung cancer in an organized health awareness assembly. School 3 will receive training in a workshop on resisting peer pressure and assertiveness techniques during physical education classes. Each condition will require about one hour of school time. Each student that participates must have written permission from the parent. All students are pretested and posttested, using a Smoking Behavior and Interest Inventory.

(D) **Compare Teen Sex Education Interventions.** Intermediate schools and high schools located in the northeast region of Fresno will implement a social inoculation training curriculum which involves role-playing and discussions about real-life sexual dilemmas and pressures that adolescents typically confront. Intermediate school and high schools located in the south region of town will institute a program, which involves classes hosting guest speakers who relay personal accounts of their experiences. These speakers would include a person suffering from AIDS, a teenage mother, a teenager who contracted a sexually transmitted disease, a teenager who gave birth to an infant suffering the effects of fetal alcohol syndrome, etc. All of the other intermediate and high schools in the Fresno school district will merely have group discussions about sexuality, facilitated by a science teacher. All of the adolescents will be administered a survey, entitled Sexual Attitudes and Behavior Inventory, both before and after they participate in their assigned curriculum.

3. **Identify Type I and Type II Errors.** For the following four examples (A, B, C, and D), identify the given scenario as either a potential Type I or Type II error. Explain your decision by referring to the definitions of Type I and Type II errors. Comment on the seriousness of committing a Type I or Type II error.

(A) Investigators are researching a **new vaccine to prevent the onset of AIDS in HIV positive subjects.** One hundred HIV positive subjects volunteered to participate. Half of the subjects (N=50) were randomly assigned to Condition 1, which received the experimental vaccine, while the other half (N=50) were assigned to Condition 2, which received a placebo. Medically the vaccine results looked very encouraging, but statistically significant differences between the groups were not attained. The researchers failed to reject the null hypothesis (p <.01), and the public is denied possible treatment.

(B) Educational consultants were hired by a progressive California school district to study **the effectiveness of competitive vs. cooperative learning.** The school district was known for its highly competitive philosophy, for which it was criticized despite its successful student test scores on national assessments. The educational consultants researched several school districts nationwide and in Japan. They found that school districts that operated with a cooperative model had significantly higher test scores and higher student satisfaction than the competitive schools (i.e., investigators rejected the null hypothesis). The competitive school district is strongly considering a bond measure in the next election to fund a change to the cooperative model with estimated costs of approximately 250 million dollars.

(C) **Silicone breast implants** have been popular for many years for purposes of breast reconstruction and breast enlargement. Since no evidence had been collected by the drug manufacturing company nor the public, it was incorrectly assumed that they presented no harm to public health (i.e., failure to reject the null hypothesis). Currently, due to reports of serious complications from thousands of women who elected to have this surgery, silicone implants are no longer being produced by major drug manufacturers.

(D) In the 1930's, surgical procedures in which the neural connection between the prefrontal lobes was severed were performed frequently. **Lobotomies** were used on chronically hospitalized mental patients. It was considered a quick and easy treatment for mental disorders. The null hypothesis was incorrectly rejected. We now know that lobotomized patients may sink into a confused stupor or become vegetable-like. Today, lobotomies are rarely performed in psychological clinical practice.

4. **Critical Thinking About Science.** What are three examples of questions that science can not address? Why is science not applicable to these questions?

5. **Public Perception of Science.**

   A. Interview three people in the general public (e.g., family members) on their perceptions of science. Record their impressions on the following questions:

      1.   What is science?
      2.   What does a scientist look like?
      3.   What do scientists do?
      4.   Name one scientist.
      5.   How important is science in advancing technological progress?

B. Write a reflective paragraph that addresses the following focus questions:

1. Were you surprised about the public's perception of science?
2. Do you see any similarities between public perception and what you have learned about science in this class?
3. In general, do people have a positive or negative impression of science?

C. Find a famous quote on InfoTrac about the contribution of science to progress or improving the quality of life.

RESEARCH SUMMARY AND DISCUSSION QUESTIONS

Testing the Hypothesis: A Conceptual Introduction

Gibson, E. J., & Walk, R. D. (1960). The visual cliff. *Scientific American, 202*, 67-71.

In Chapter 7, Ray introduced the concept of confounds and threats to internal validity in experimentation. These threats are especially problematic when participants are exposed to more than one experimental condition. In Gibson and Walk's study on depth perception, infants aged 6 to 14 months were exposed to two experimental conditions. To test depth perception, a visual cliff device was utilized. This device is a glass table under which there is a solid checkered surface; however, on one side the solid surface is directly under the glass top (i.e., the shallow side) and on the other side the solid surface is at floor level (i.e., the deep side) creating a visual cliff. In the first experimental condition, infants were placed in the center of the visual cliff and summoned by their mother to crawl to deep side of the table. Most infants refused to crawl to the deep side. Next, infants were placed again in the center of the visual cliff and called by their mothers to the shallow side. Significantly more infants crawled to the shallow side. Thus, the investigators concluded that infants perceive depth early in life.

Discussion Questions
1. Discuss potential threats to validity in this study.
2. Did this study prove that depth perception is innate in humans?
3. In this study, what is the probability that a Type I error was made?

SUGGESTED READING

Huck, S. W., & Sandler, H. M. (1979). *Rival hypotheses: Alternative explanations of data based conclusions.* New York: Harper & Row.

This book provides great examples to practice identifying hypotheses and confounds.

ANSWERS

Fill-in: Self Test
1. Internal validity
2. Chance
3. Null
4. Confounds
5. Control
6. Secondary variance
7. Error
8. Treatment effect
9. Type II error
10. Selection
11. Hypothesis
12. Self-correcting
13. Diffusion
14. Effect size
15. Treatment

True/False: Self Test
1. True
2. True
3. False
4. False
5. False
6. True
7. True
8. False
9. True
10. True

Multiple Choice: Self Test

1. D
2. B
3. D
4. E
5. B
6. B
7. B
8. A
9. A
10. A
11. D
12. C
13. B
14. B
15. D
16. D
17. B

CHAPTER 7

Control: Keystone of the Experimental Method

CHAPTER OBJECTIVES: CONCEPT CHECKS

The chapter objectives provide you with a concept checklist. These are things you should know after reading Chapter 7. The accompanying text page numbers are reference aids for your review.

1. Explain why the experimental framework requires one to interpret experimental results in terms of not one but three separate hypotheses. (147)

2. How is control the keystone to the experimental method? (147)

3. How does control apply to participant assignment, experimental design, and the logic of experimentation? (147-153)

4. What is the objective of random selection? How is it performed? (149)

5. How does random selection (sampling) differ from random assignment? (149-155)

6. Distinguish between equating, counterbalancing, and randomization as methods of participant assignment. (149-155)

7. What are the advantages and disadvantages of pretesting? How does the Solomon four-group design assess the effects related to pretesting? (156-158)

8. Summarize the four conceptual steps in experimentation. (159)

9. What functions must the experimental design perform? How is the experimental design like a blueprint? (155)

10. In the pretest-posttest control group design, which threats to internal validity are controlled and which are not? (156-157)

11. What are the three main characteristics of a true experiment? (167)

12. Describe how confounds influence experimental interpretations. (160)

STUDY GUIDE AND REVIEW

Key Terms

Define each of these terms in your own words. Check your understanding of Chapter 7 by referring to the featured text page.

1. Control (154)

2. Random selection (157)

3. Random number table (157)

4. Equating procedure (158)

5. Elimination procedure (158)

6. Counterbalancing (159)

7. Randomization (160-161)

8. Random sampling (161)

9. Random assignment (161-162)

10. Representative (161)

11. Experimental design (162)

12. Posttest-only control group design (163)

13. Pretest (163)

14. Posttest (163)

15. Pretest-posttest control group design (163)

16. Solomon four-group design (165)

17. True experiment (164-165)

Fill-in: Self Test

Fill in the missing word or phrase. Focus your attention on important Chapter 7 details.

1. When we reject the null hypothesis, we want to be certain the differences between groups are due to the independent variable and not to other factors known as _____. (154)

2. _____ and manipulation allow us to examine individual variables in detail and determine the influence of one variable on another. (154)

3. Artificial environments for experiments may not mirror the world. This is a problem that threatens _____. (154)

4. In _____, every member in the potential participant pool has an equal chance of being chosen as a participant. (161)

5. The goal of random sampling is to select a sample that is _____ of the population. (161)

6. ECCE represents a commonly used _____ procedure that ensures each condition precedes and follows the other condition an equal number of times. (159)

7. To distribute potential confounds between groups, one of our most powerful tools is _____. (160-161)

8. A(n) _____ is a table of numbers ordered in such a manner that their occurrence cannot be predicted with a mathematical formula. (156-157)

9. _____ refers to the assignment of selected participants to groups -- for example, an experimental and a control group. (161-162)

10. The basic idea behind randomization is to leave the assignment of participants to a group solely to _____. (161)

11. A sound _____ will allow us to determine the effect of the independent variable on the dependent variable and to rule out alternative explanations. (162)

12.	Group 1	Pretest	Treatment	Posttest
	Group 2	Pretest	Control	Posttest
	Group 3		Treatment	Posttest
	Group 4			Posttest

This experimental design is called _____ design. (164)

13. The effects of _____ variables may cause greater within-group variance thus making it more difficult to reject the null hypothesis. (167)

14. A simple rule for _____ is to achieve as much control as possible over the experimental situation and to use this control to make the experiment as similar as possible for all participants. (167)

True/False: Self Test

Test your understanding of Chapter 7 by marking the best answer to these true or false items.

1. _____ Ultimately, the conceptual and practical goal of experimentation is to understand the influence the independent variable has on the dependent variable. (154)

2. _____ Technically, there are a number of ways to randomly sample. (158)

3. _____ Random selection helps to ensure that participants reflect the population. (158))

4. _____ An advantage of assigning an equal number of male and female participants to conditions is that it eliminates sex differences. (158)

5. _____ Assigning participants to either of two groups by flipping a coin is an example of randomization. (161)

6. _____ Randomization is a powerful technique with many advantages; however, it can not control for unknown potentially confounding variables. (161)

7. _____ Randomization randomizes everything to remove the differences between the individuals in our experimental groups. (61)

8. _____ The quality of experimental answers is influenced by several factors. The most important is the structure or experimental design we use to seek answers. (162)

9. _____ Rating your control group before the experimental group strengthens internal validity by stabilizing your instrumentation prior to measurement of participants in the treatment condition. (164)

10. _____ Between-group variance is influenced solely by the differences between groups due to the manipulation of the independent variable. (166)

Multiple Choice: Self Test

Test your Chapter 7 comprehension by circling the best answer to these multiple choice questions.

1. What is an important consideration in interpretation of the experimental results? (154)

    a. The chance hypothesis
    b. The confound hypothesis
    c. The research hypothesis
    d. All of the above

2. Decisions about how many participants to use in experimentation are dependent upon _____. (155)

    a. the research question being asked
    b. information presented in relevant literature
    c. the number of participants used in similar or related experiments
    d. All of the above

3. Assigning equal numbers of men and women to each experimental condition is an example of _____. (158)

    a. proportional assignment
    b. counterbalancing
    c. an equating procedure
    d. random assignment

4. The most powerful technique to distribute confounds between groups is _____. (160-161)

    a. counterbalancing
    b. matching
    c. equating
    d. randomization

5. A simple rule in experimentation is that the more consistently participants are treated, the smaller the _____ variance. (167)

    a. between-groups
    b. within-groups
    c. total
    d. All of the above

6. In the randomly assigned pretest-posttest control group design what threat(s) to internal validity (is/are) controlled for? (163-164)

    a. History
    b. Maturation
    c. Testing
    d. Statistical regression
    e. All of the above

7. If extraneous variables affect both groups, then the within-groups variance is increased, making it more difficult to _____ the null hypothesis. (167)

    a. accept
    b. reject
    c. fail to reject
    d. prove

8. In the Solomon four-group design, what conditions are presented in Group 3? (164-165)

    a. Pretest-Treatment-Posttest
    b. Treatment-Posttest
    c. Pretest-Control-Posttest
    d. Posttest

9. By using the Solomon four-group design, the experimenter is able to determine _____. (164-165)

    a. the effects of the treatment
    b. the interaction of the treatment with the presence or absence of the pretest
    c. the effects of history
    d. All of the above

10. What are the characteristics of a true experiment according to Campbell and Stanley (1968)? (165)

    a. Random assignment of participants to groups
    b. At least two levels of an independent variable
    c. Control for threats to validity
    d. All of the above

11. An example of a counterbalancing procedure is _____. (159)

    a. CECE
    b. ECEC
    c. ECCE
    d. None of the above

12. One way to ensure that our sample is representative and conclusions have external and ecological validity is to _____. (161-162)

    a. equate groups
    b. counterbalance
    c. randomly sample
    d. randomly assign to treatment conditions

13. What controls for both known and unknown potentially confounding variables? (161)

    a. Random sample
    b. Random assignment
    c. Effect size
    d. Power

14. The ratio of between group variance to within group variance is___. (166)

    a. power
    b. Type I error
    c. Type II error
    d. F-ratio

15. An important criterion to generalize our experimental conclusions beyond the participants in our study is _____. (161)

    a. a representative sample
    b. random assignment
    c. control
    d. pretest/post-test design

<u>Essays</u>

Apply your knowledge of Chapter 7 as you analyze the following questions in detail. Specifically refer to information in the chapter to support your answers.

1. Discuss how control is achieved through participant selection and participant assignment. Discuss the practical use of the random number table in this process.

2. Discuss the advantages of using random sampling and random assignment.

3. How is control achieved through experimental design? What are the objectives of a sound experimental design?

4. Review Campbell and Stanley's (1963) threats to internal validity in Chapter 6. How can each threat be controlled?

5. Identify the limitations associated with the pretest-posttest control group design.

6. What are the characteristics of a true experiment?

7. Apply a Solomon four-group design to test the effects of mentoring at-risk youth to improve their motivation to achieve. Why is the Solomon four-group design advantageous during the interpretation of results? How does this design compare to the posttest-only control-group design and the pretest-posttest control-group design?

8. How is control related to the logic of experimentation?

9. Diagram the types of variance associated with the F-ratio. Explain how the F-ratio is related to hypothesis testing.

RESEARCH ACTIVITIES

The goals of the research activities are to: (1) relate Chapter 7 on an applied learning dimension, and (2) get you involved in research.

1. **Design a Research Flowchart.** Develop your research hypothesis from Chapter 6 into an experimental design. Your objective is to use a systematic, step-by-step process to test your hypothesis. Fill in the following information.

   Step 1: What is the research hypothesis?

   Step 2: What is the population of interest?

   Step 3: How will you sample? Estimate the needed sample size.

   Step 4: How will you assign participants to conditions?

Step 5:

        a. Manipulation of an independent variable?
            Experimental design
            Observation of differences between groups
                1. How many independent variables?
                2. How many levels of each independent variable?

        b. No manipulation of an independent variable?
            Correlational design
            Measurement of variables

Step 6: Operationally define your independent and dependent variables.

Step 7: Specify controls in your experimental design.

Step 8: What statistical analysis is planned?

Step 9: What level of alpha is selected?

Step 10: What are the expected findings?

2.   **Anorexic Patients. Random Assignment into Treatment Conditions -- Using the Random Number Table.** You are interested in investigating the effects of behavior modification therapy in the treatment of anorexia nervosa. The following participants, who have been coded to protect anonymity, are patients in the Eating Disorders Unit at the Community Hospital. Their weights and ages have been recorded. Your assignment is to randomly assign these participants to treatment conditions by using a random number table.

Objective: Randomly distribute subject characteristics between groups. Each participant should have an equal chance of being assigned to either the experimental or the control group.

Strategies Using the Random Number Table: There are many possible creative uses of the random number table. Here are two alternatives (Bordens & Abbott, 1991).

A. ODD-EVEN METHOD

  1. Use the random number table in the appendix of your text.

  2. Randomly start anywhere on the table.

  3. Assign a random digit (using single digits from the random number table) to each participant.

4. a. Assign participants who were randomly assigned odd numbers to Treatment Group 1.

   b. Assign participants who were randomly assigned even numbers to Treatment Group 2.

Note: If it is important to have the same number of participants in both groups, assign participants to Treatment Group 1 until its size equals one-half N. The remaining participants shall automatically be assigned to Treatment Group 2.

B. DIRECT METHOD

1. Use the random number table in the appendix of the text.

2. Randomly start anywhere on the table.

3. Designate numbers to represent treatment groups. For example let the number 1 represent the first treatment group, and let the number 2 represent the second treatment group.

4. Begin with the first participant and read the random numbers as single digits. As you come across either a "1" or a "2" assign that participants to the respective treatment group. Continue with the other participants.

Note: If it is important to have the same number of participants in both groups, assign participants to Treatment Group 1 until its size equals one-half N. The remaining participants shall be automatically assigned to Treatment Group 2.

DATA:

Participant	Age	Weight
A	14	88
B	17	92
C	25	99
D	21	101
E	15	79
F	18	91
G	23	95
H	21	84
I	15	82
J	16	64
K	17	79
L	18	86
M	19	87
N	13	61
O	16	74
P	20	89
Q	13	76
R	15	82
S	17	70
T	19	90
U	12	68
V	22	88
W	23	85
X	16	73
Y	18	99
Z	14	78

RANDOM ASSIGNMENT

Group 1: Behavior Modification

	Participant	Age	Weight
1.			
2.			
3.			
4.			
5.			
6.			
7.			
8.			
9.			
10.			
11.			
12.			
13.			

Group 2: Control Group

	Participant	Age	Weight
1.			
2.			
3.			
4.			
5.			
6.			
7.			
8.			
9.			
10.			
11.			
12.			
13.			

Analyze the randomly assigned groups. Use a t-test to assess whether there are significant differences between these groups in terms of weight before the behavior modification treatment begins.

3. **Identify Experimental Designs:**

    a. Investigators are interested in the affects of **caffeine on Premenstrual Syndrome (PMS).** Patients are randomly assigned to one of two conditions. Group 1 will be allowed to consume unlimited amounts of caffeine during a one-month period. Group 2 requires that patients will agree not to consume any caffeine products as specified in a written contract. At the end of the month-long study severity of PMS symptoms will be assessed.

        Questions:
        1. What kind of experimental design is illustrated?
        2. What is the independent variable?
        3. What is the dependent variable?
        4. Diagram this design.
        5. What are the potential confounds?

    b. Investigators are interested in the **ability of computer technology to enhance visualization to promote T-cell production in children with cancer.** Patients are randomly assigned to one of two conditions. Group 1 patients will receive a new computer visualization program that instructs the children to visualize the action of healing cells in their body which are aggressively fighting their cancer. Group 2 patients will not receive the computer program nor any visualization training. Before treatment begins, all patients' T-cell levels will be measured via blood tests. The experimental and control treatment conditions will be initiated, and the experiment is planned to proceed for three months. After three months all patients' T-cell levels will again be measured from blood samples.

        Questions:
        1. What kind of experimental design is illustrated?
        2. What is the independent variable?
        3. What is the dependent variable?
        4. Diagram this design.
        5. What are the potential confounds?

    c. Investigators are interested in the effect of **positive self-statements on the self-esteem of women diagnosed with Battered Woman's Syndrome.** All subjects will be randomly assigned to four groups. Group 1 will be given a self-esteem inventory prior to treatment. Subjects will then be instructed to use specific positive self-statements twice each day at determined times. The program will continue for four weeks. At the end of the four-week program each subject's self-esteem will be assessed, using the same self-esteem inventory previously administered. Group 2 will also be given a self-esteem inventory to determine a baseline measure. Subjects in this condition will not receive the positive self-statement treatment nor any other treatment. After four weeks subjects will be reassessed on the original self-esteem inventory. Group 3 will receive positive self-statement training for four weeks and then will be administered the self-esteem inventory. Group 4 will be administered the self-esteem inventory at the end of the four experimental weeks. The self-esteem of all subjects will be compared to assess for treatment effects, pretest sensitization and history effects.

Questions:
1. What kind of experimental design is illustrated?
2. What is the independent variable?
3. What is the dependent variable?
4. Diagram this design.
5. What are the potential confounds?

4. **Improving Pro-environmental Behaviors of Students.**
Develop an educational intervention to improve the pro-environmental behaviors of primary school students. Apply one of the experimental designs presented in Chapter 7. Summarize the investigation and address the following questions. Show all your work in your workbook.

Questions:
1. What kind of experimental design is illustrated?
2. What is the independent variable?
3. What is the dependent variable?
4. Diagram this design.
5. What are the potential confounds?

5. **Application of Classic Experimental Studies.** Use InfoTrac to discover if any experimental studies have been used as evidence to change legislation or public policy.

RESEARCH SUMMARY AND DISCUSSION QUESTIONS

Control: The Keystone of the Experimental Method

Festinger, L. & Carlsmith, J. M. (1959). Cognitive consequences of forced compliance. *Journal of Abnormal and Social Psychology, 58*, 203-210.

Ray, in Chapter 7 of the text, emphasized the importance of control in the experimental method. One way to achieve control is to randomly assign participants to experimental conditions. Festinger and Carlsmith used random assignment to examine cognitive dissonance in this classic experiment.

After completing a series of boring and tedious tasks, participants were randomly assigned to one of three conditions. In condition 1, participants were offered one dollar to lie to other participants about the boring tasks and to describe the tasks as enjoyable, interesting, and fun. In condition 2, participants were offered $20 to lie and make positive statements about the tasks. And in condition 3, the control group, participants were not told to lie and no money was offered.

The findings of this study were counterintuitive. Those participants who were paid $1 later reported that they liked the boring tasks more than those who were paid $20 or those who were not told to lie. This supports the theory of cognitive dissonance, which predicted that participants who had very little incentive would report greater attitude change than those who had a large incentive or no incentive.

Discussion Questions

1.   Discuss how random assignment strengthened control in this experiment.
2.   Show how control was achieved through experimental design. Follow Ray's format and diagram this experimental design.

SUGGESTED READINGS

Campbell, D. T., & Stanley, J. C. (1963). *Experimental and quasi-experimental designs for research*. Chicago: Rand McNally.

An important reference on confounds and threats to internal validity.

Solomon, R. L. (1949). On extension of control group design. *Psychological Bulletin, 46*, 137-150.

More from the founder of the Solomon four-group design.

ANSWERS

Fill-in: Self test
1.   Confounds
2.   Control
3.   External validity
4.   Random sampling
5.   Representative
6.   Counterbalancing
7.   Randomization
8.   Random number table
9.   Random assignment
10. Chance
11. Experimental design
12. Solomon four-group
13. Extraneous
14. Internal validity

True/False: Self Test
1. True
2. True
3. True
4. False
5. True
6. False
7. False
8. True
9. False
10. False

Multiple Choice: Self Test
1. D
2. D
3. C
4. D
5. B
6. E
7. B
8. B
9. D
10. D
11. C
12. D
13. B
14. D
15. A

CHAPTER 8

Applying the Logic of Experimentation: Between-Subjects Design

CHAPTER OBJECTIVES: CONCEPT CHECKS

The chapter objectives provide you with a concept checklist. These are things you should know after reading Chapter 8. The accompanying text page numbers are reference aids for your review.

1. What are the characteristics of a between-subjects design? (172)

2. What is the simplest between-subjects design? Describe this design. (173)

3. What are the features of a multilevel, completely randomized design? (173-174)

4. What are post hoc tests and when are they used? (177)

5. What are the objectives of a priori tests? (177)

6. What are the defining features of a factorial design? (178)

7. How many hypotheses are analyzed in a 2 X 2 factorial design? How many F-ratios are calculated in a 2 X 2 factorial design? (188-195)

8. Describe an analysis of variance F-table. (186-187)

9. What is an interaction in factorial design? How does it influence the experimental interpretation? What does it look like graphically? (182-187)

10. Why is it a problem to use subject variables in factorial designs to make causal interpretations? (195-197)

11. What are the advantages of the factorial design? (197)

STUDY GUIDE AND REVIEW

<u>**Key Terms**</u>

Define each of these terms in your own words. Check your understanding of Chapter 8 by referring to the featured text page.

1. Between-subjects design (172)

2. Within-subjects design (172)

3. Completely randomized design (173)

4. Multilevel completely randomized design (173-174)

5. Single factor analysis of variance (177)

6. Post hoc tests (177)

7. A priori tests (177)

8. Factorial designs (178)

9. Factors (179)

10. Main effects (180)

11. Interaction effect (180)

12. Cells (180)

13. Matrix (183)

14. Mean square (186-187)

15. Subject variable (195)

Fill-in: Self Test

Fill in the missing word or phrase. Focus your attention on important Chapter 8 details.

1. A general class of designs in which different subjects are used in each experimental group describes _____. (172)

2. An alternative to the between-subjects design is a design in which subjects are exposed to all levels of a factor. This is called _____. (172)

3. Multilevel experimental designs refer to more than two levels of the _____. (173)

4. After rejecting the null hypotheses, one may apply _____ tests to compare the differences between groups taken as pairs. (177)

5. Comparisons planned before a study is performed are referred to as _____ tests. (177)

6. A design that allows examination of the effects of more than one independent variable, both individually and collectively, is the _____. (178)

7. In factorial designs the independent variables are also referred to as _____. (179)

8. In a factorial diagram the blocks are called _____. (180)

9. In a 6 X 2 factorial design there are _____ independent variables. (182)

10. In a 3 X 6 factorial design there are _____ separate cells. (182)

11. In a 2 X 2 between-subjects factorial design each subject receives _____ level(s) of each of the independent variables. (182)

12. The treatment differences in a factorial design are referred to as _____. (180)

13. In factorial design, when the independent variables combine in various ways to affect the dependent variable, these combined effects are referred to as _____. (180)

14. A _____ variable (ex. gender) is a characteristic or condition that a participant is seen to possess in a relatively permanent manner. (195)

15. In a _____ design, main effects and interactions are assessed simultaneously. (182)

True/False: Self Test

Test your understanding of Chapter 8 by marking the best answer to these true or false items.

1. _____Between-subjects designs are a general class of designs in which the same subjects are used in each group. (172)

2. _____One characteristic of the between-subjects design is that each subject receives all levels of the independent variable. (172)

3. _____ Post hoc tests are utilized when no statistical significance is found. (177)

4. _____ Randomization is not used in between-subjects designs. (174)

5. _____ Subject characteristics should be interpreted cautiously in experimental design, since there is no random assignment of characteristics. (179)

6. _____ In a 2 X 3 X 4 factorial design there are 24 independent variables. (180)

7. _____ In a summary table of results for between-subjects experimental designs, the column that represents the variance attributable to treatment effects and error is designated "p." (187)

8. _____ In hypothesis testing, the basis for rejecting the null hypothesis is the "p" probability. (187)

9. _____ Parallel lines in graphs of factorial results indicate a nonsignificant interaction. (192)

10. _____ In a 2X2 factorial design there are eight possible outcomes, including main effects and interactions. (188)

Multiple Choice: Self Test

Test your Chapter 8 comprehension by circling the best answer to these multiple choice questions.

1.   A distinctive feature of the between-subjects design is that it _____. (172)

    a. examines the effects of more than one independent variable
    b. examines the effects of more than one dependent variable
    c. involves the comparison between different groups of participants
    d. involves the comparison between the same group of participants

2.   This experimental design indicates that the assignment of subjects was _____. (173)

R	Group A	T (High Level)	M
R	Group B	T (Zero Level)	M

    a. completely recorded
    b. completely randomized
    c. completely counterbalanced
    d. All of the above

3.   Research from the example in the text investigating the effects of four varying amounts of coffee on the flying skills of airline pilots applies the _____. (173)

    a. 2 X 2 completely randomized design
    b. multilevel completely randomized design
    c. Solomon four-group design
    d. pretest-posttest control group design

4.   The dependent variable in the above example was _____. (173)

    a. the number of cups of coffee
    b. flight simulator vs. no flight simulator
    c. number of flying errors
    d. airline pilots

5.   The most common way to analyze a single-factor completely randomized design is _____. (177)

    a. correlation
    b. post hoc tests
    c. single-factor ANOVA
    d. factorial analysis of variance

6. What is an important statistical prerequisite for applying post hoc tests? (177)

   a. $p > .01$
   b. $p > .05$
   c. Reject the null hypothesis
   d. Retain the null hypothesis

7. What are the defining characteristic(s) of this experimental design? (174)

R	Group 1	M	T1	M
R	Group 2	M	T2	M
R	Group 3	M	T3	M

   a. Completely randomized
   b. Pretest/Posttest
   c. Multilevel
   d. All of the above

8. What is the difference between factorial designs and single-factor designs? (178)

   a. Factorial designs examine the effects of more than one independent variable
   b. Factorial designs assess multiple dependent variables
   c. Factorial designs examine the interaction between variables
   d. Both a and c

9. In analyzing a 2 X 2 factorial design, how many F-ratios are calculated? (186)
   a. 1
   b. 2
   c. 3
   d. 4

10. In analyzing the results of a two factor design, what do you interpret first? (180)

   a. The main effect of Factor A
   b. The main effect of Factor B
   c. The interaction effect
   d. The parallel effect

11. When the lines intersect on a line graph representing the results of a factorial design, this indicates _____ . (190)

    a. significant main effects
    b. a significant interaction effect
    c. nonsignificant main effects
    d. a nonsignificant interaction effect

12. If you read that scientists had just found significant differences in the size of the hypothalamus of homosexual men as compared to heterosexual men, then you could accurately conclude that _____ . (193)

    a. the differences are due to homosexuality
    b. the differences may be due to a third variable such as hormonal imbalance
    c. establishing causality is difficult because the given subject characteristics were not randomly assigned
    d. Both b and c

13. In a 2 X 2 factorial design there are _____. (180)

    a. two independent variables
    b. two main effects
    c. interaction effects
    d. All of the above

14. Which of the following is a subject variable? (195)

    a. ethnicity
    b. how many cups of coffee you consume
    c. weight
    d. All of the above

15. In assessing the outcome of a factorial design graphically you notice intersecting lines. What does this suggest? (192)

    a. main effects.
    b. no main effects
    c. interaction effects
    d. no interaction effect

<u>Essays</u>

Apply your knowledge of Chapter 8 as you analyze the following questions in detail. Specifically refer to information in the chapter to support your answers.

1. Compare and contrast the single-level between-subjects design, the multilevel between-subjects design, and the factorial design. Schematically diagram each and address appropriate inferential statistics for each.

2. Discuss the role of a priori tests and post hoc tests in hypothesis testing. Give examples where each may be used.

3. In regards to a factorial design, discuss the difference between main effects and interaction effects. Also explain the order in which these effects should be interpreted. Depict each of these effects pictorially and explain the graphs drawn.

4. When a researcher reports that the F-ratio is statistically significant, how should this be interpreted? When should post hoc tests be applied?

5. Why must investigators be especially cautious in interpreting subject variables in factorial designs? Give an example that illustrates this problem.

6. Describe and provide a schematic diagram for a 3 x 2 x 4 factorial design. How many factors, levels of each factor, and cells are there in this example?

7. Discuss the advantages of factorial analysis versus performing separate single-level analyses.

RESEARCH ACTIVITIES

The goals of the research activities are to: (1) relate Chapter 8 on an applied learning dimension, and (2) get you involved in research.

1. **Dirty Words, Alcohol and Memory. Factorial Analysis of Variance**

    a. Using the data provided below, fill in the missing information on the summary table.

    b. Graph the results, using a line graph.

    c. Interpret the findings.

This hypothetical study investigated the effect of alcohol (no alcohol versus strong alcohol) on the ability of 20 introductory psychology students to correctly recall either a list of non-dirty words or a list of highly dirty words. All participants were randomly assigned to conditions. This design was 2 X 2 and completely randomized. The dependent variable was the number of repetitions required for perfect recall.

A1B1 Strong Alcohol/ Non-Dirty Words	A2B1 No Alcohol/ Non-Dirty Words
21	19
22	20
19	18
18	17
21	21

A1B2 Strong Alcohol/ Highly Dirty Words	A2B2 No Alcohol/ Highly Dirty Words
2	7
5	7
6	5
3	6
4	8

A.

SUMMARY TABLE

Source of Variance	SS	df	MS	F
A				
B				
A X B				
Error				
Total				

B. Graph

C. Report your findings

D. Interpret

2. **Fasting and Meditation: Effects on Spiritual Awareness. 3 X 2 Factorial Design.** What are the effects of fasting and meditation on spiritual awareness? Levels of fasting were manipulated using 3 conditions (long term, semi-long term, and short term). Levels of meditation were manipulated using 2 conditions (high and none). Participants self-reported their spiritual awareness.

Each of these experiments represents a different potential outcome. Graph and interpret the results using the cell means presented in the following tables. Indicate if there appear to be main effects or an interaction between fasting and meditation on spiritual awareness.

Experiment I

| | Fasting Level | | |
	Long term	Semi-Long term	Short term
High	40	50	60
None	40	50	60

Experiment II

| | Fasting Level | | |
	Long term	Semi-Long term	Short term
High	50	50	50
None	60	60	60

Experiment III

| | Fasting Level | | |
	Long term	Semi-Long term	Short term
High	60	70	80
None	80	70	60

Experiment IV

| | Fasting Level | | |
	Long term	Semi-Long term	Short term
High	40	50	60
None	70	80	90

Experiment V

| | Fasting Level | | |
	Long term	Semi-Long term	Short term
High	50	60	70
None	60	60	60

Experiment VI

	Fasting Level		
	Long term	Semi-Long term	Short term
High	40	50	60
None	80	70	60

Experiment VII

	Fasting Level		
	Long term	Semi-Long term	Short term
High	60	80	100
None	50	60	70

3. **Predicting Main Effects and Interactions in Factorial Designs.** Refer to Box 8.1 (Bower, Monteiro, and Gilligan, 1978) in your text. Predict if there is a main effect for factor A, mood during memory recall, a main effect for factor B, mood as list was learned, and an interaction effect between these variables on percentage of words remembered.

4. **Interpreting Cause and Effect.** Which of the following has the potential to yield cause and effect results? Explain your reasoning.

   a. Effect of paternal abuse on ADD
   b. Effect of cigarette smoking on lung cancer in humans
   c. Effect of premature birth on learning disabilities
   d. Effect of hypothalamus size on male sexual orientation

5. **Critical Thinking about Experiments.** View the movie *Ghostbusters*. Compare and contrast the experimental method in Chapter 8 with the procedures in this movie. Find other articles on Infotrac about paranormal studies. Write an essay explaining your comparative observations.

RESEARCH SUMMARY AND DISCUSSION QUESTIONS

Applying the Logic of Experimentation: Between-Subjects Designs

   Bandura, A., Ross, D., & Ross, S.A. (1961). Transmission of aggression through imitation of aggressive models. *Journal of Abnormal and Social Psychology, 63*, 575-582.

   This classic experiment exemplifies factorial design as highlighted in Chapter 8. In the "Bobo doll" experiment, Bandura examined the impact of social modeling on aggressive behavior.

Preschool children were first randomly assigned to either an aggressive, nonaggressive, or control group. In the aggressive experimental condition, children observed an adult verbally and physically aggress against an inflated doll (i.e., a Bobo doll). In the nonaggressive condition, children observed an adult acting nonaggresively towards the Bobo doll, and in the control condition children were not exposed to any behavioral model. Secondly, male and female participants were divided into groups. Finally, children were randomly assigned so that half were exposed to same-sex models and half to opposite-sex models. Thus, the factors in this study were the type of modeling (i.e., aggressive versus nonaggressive), the gender of participant (i.e., male versus female), and the gender of aggressive model (i.e., same-sex versus opposite sex). The dependent variable was the aggressive behavior of children toward the Bobo doll.

First, it was found that children who were exposed to aggressive modeling imitated aggression. Secondly, boys were more aggressive than girls. Finally, children were more aggressive when they were exposed to an aggressive model of the same sex. Thus, this research clearly demonstrated the effect of adult modeling on children's behavior.

Discussion Questions
1. What are the hypotheses in this study?
2. Interpret the main effects and the interaction effects in this study.
3. Explain the advantages of this design.

SUGGESTED READINGS

Ebbinghaus, H. (1964). *Memory* (1885/1913). New York: Dover.

   For further information on memory refer to this classic work.

Marschark, M., & Hunt, R. R. (1989). A reexamination of the role of imagery in learning and memory. *Journal of Experimental Psychology: Learning, Memory, and Cognition, 15*, 710-720.

   Explores the importance of imagery in memory.

ANSWERS

Fill-in: Self Test
1. Between-subjects designs
2. Within-subjects design
3. Independent variable
4. Post hoc
5. A priori
6. Factorial design
7. Factors
8. Cells
9. 2
10. 18
11. 1
12. Main effects
13. Interaction effects
14. subject
15. factorial

True/False: Self Test
1. False
2. False
3. False
4. False
5. True
6. False
7. False
8. True
9. True
10. True

Multiple Choice: Self Test

1. C
2. B
3. B
4. C
5. C
6. C
7. D
8. D
9. C
10. C
11. B
12. D
13. E
14. A
15. C

CHAPTER 9

Extending the Logic of Experimentation:
Within-Subjects and Matched Subjects Approaches

CHAPTER OBJECTIVES: CONCEPT CHECKS

The chapter objectives provide you with a concept checklist. These are things you should know after reading Chapter 9. The accompanying text page numbers are reference aids for your review.

1. What are the defining characteristics of the within-subjects design? How is this design different from a between-subjects design? (201)

2. What is the role of random assignment in within-subjects design? (201)

3. How is the within-subjects design more sensitive in terms of decreasing the chance of error variance? (203)

4. With respect to error variance in the F-ratio, how does this term differ in the within-subjects design compared to the between-subjects design? (203)

5. All other things being equal, which is more sensitive to changes in the treatments, the between-subjects design or the within-subjects design? (206)

6. What is carryover and how does it confound the within-subjects design? (206)

7. How can carryover be controlled in the within-subjects design? (206)

8. Under what conditions is the within-subjects design not an appropriate design? (206-208)

9. What conditions must be met for complete counterbalancing? (207)

10. How is the repeated measures design used to study the process of learning or practice effects directly in the within-subjects design? (208)

11. What are the characteristics of a mixed design? (209-210)

12. What are the advantages of using a matched-subjects procedure? (211-212)

13. Explain the process of matching subjects. (211-212)

14. Why is the relationship between the variable used for matching and the dependent variable important in order for matching to work? (212)

15. Describe the randomized block design. (213-214)

16. With respect to matching, distinguish between the terms blocking, stratifying and leveling. (215)

STUDY GUIDE AND REVIEW

<u>Key Terms</u>

Define each of these terms in your own words. Check your understanding of Chapter 9 by referring to the featured text page.

1. Within-subjects design (201)

2. Carryover (206

3. Order effects (206-207)

4. Counterbalancing (205)

5. Intrasubject counterbalancing (204)

6. Fatigue effects (207)

7. Practice effects (206-207)

8. Complete counterbalancing (207)

9. Incomplete counterbalancing (207)

10. .Differential order effect (208)

11. Treatment by order interaction (208)

12. Repeated measures (208)

13. Mixed designs (209)

14. Matched subjects (211)

15. Randomized block design (213)

16. Blocking (215)

17. Stratifying (215)

18. Leveling (215)

Fill-in: Self Test

Fill in the missing word or phrase. Focus your attention on important Chapter 9 details.

1. An experimental design in which the performance of one group of participants is compared with the performance of a different, unrelated group of participants is referred to as a(n) _____. (201)

2. A design in which every participant serves in every group and receives all levels of the independent variable is called a(n) _____. (201)

3. A within-subjects design increases the sensitivity of a study by decreasing the _____ variance. (203)

4. Due to the power of the within-subjects design, smaller treatment differences are adequate for the _____ of the null hypothesis. (204)

5. Carryover is a potential problem that may seriously confound the within-subjects design and threaten _____. (206)

6. One way to control for potential order effects in the within-subjects design is to _____. (207)

7. When the effects of the treatment are dependent upon the order of presentation, this refers to _____ interaction. (208)

8. A design useful in studying psychological processes that occur over time is called _____. (208)

9. A common design in psychological research, which combines a between-subjects design with a within-subjects design, is called a(n)_____. (209)

10. Pairing participants along some factor and then randomly assigning one participant at a time to each of the two groups describes _____. (211)

11. Height, weight, and intelligence are examples of characteristics that can be used for _____. (212)

12. When the matching factor is analyzed, the resulting design is traditionally referred to as a(n) _____ design. (213)

13. Glass and Stanley (1970) suggest that the term _____ be used for cases in which matching takes place on an interval or ratio scale. (215)

14. A decline in performance due to repetition is called _____ effect. (207)

15. An improved performance due to repetition is called _____ effect. (207)

True/False: Self Test

Test your understanding of Chapter 9 by marking the better answer to these true or false items.

1. _____ There are times when random assignment is not the most appropriate experimental approach. (201)

2. _____ In a within-subjects design, performance on the dependent variable is compared following different treatments on the same set of participants. (201)

3. _____ In a within-subjects design the participant's own performance is the basis for comparison between conditions. (201)

4. _____ Since the same participants are used in each group, we can be certain that before any treatment has been presented the groups are exactly the same. (201)

5. _____ Technically, the within-subjects design reduces the variability of scores in each condition. (203)

6. _____ The error variance term in the F-ratio for within-subjects design is smaller than that of comparable between-subjects designs. (203)

7. _____ All matched-subjects designs use twins because it is inappropriate to match on a single subject factor. (211)

8. _____ In the matched-subjects schematic diagram, M before R denotes that participants were first randomly assigned. (212)

9. _____ In matching as a control procedure, participants are matched according to subject variables, but the factor is not analyzed. (212)

10. _____ When matching takes place on an ordinal scale, this is called blocking. (215)

Multiple Choice: Self Test

Test your Chapter 9 comprehension by circling the best answer to these multiple choice questions.

1. What experimental design uses random assignment alone to equate groups? (201)

   a. Between-subjects design
   b. Within-subjects design
   c. Matched-subjects design
   d. Both b and c

2. Which of the following is true of a within-subjects design? (203)

   a. Accomplishes equating groups before presentation of the independent variable
   b. Accomplishes reduction of error variance
   c. Internal validity may be threatened by carryover effects
   d. All of the above
   e. Both a and b

3. Which of the following describes an advantage of the within-subjects design? (205-206)

   a. Total number of participants can be dramatically reduced
   b. It is more sensitive than the between-subjects design
   c. It is most appropriate when the treatment has a lasting effect
   d. All of the above
   e. Both a and b

4. Which of the following is a disadvantage of the within subjects design? (206)

   a. Some questions can not be answered by a within-subjects design
   b. Carryover may confound the design
   c. Exposing participants to repeated treatment conditions may result in a decline in performance
   d. All of the above
   e. Both a and b

5. In the within-subjects design, what procedure controls for the effects of treatment order? (207)

   a. Randomization
   b. Matching
   c. Counterbalancing
   d. Blocking

6. What procedure controls for differential order effects? (208)

    a. Complete counterbalancing
    b. Intragroup counterbalancing
    c. Intrasubject counterbalancing
    d. None of the above

7. In the completely counterbalanced design, as the number of conditions increase, _____ participants are required. (207)

    a. fewer
    b. more
    c. matched
    d. blocked

8. What is the first task in the matched-subjects design? (211)

    a. Pair participants by using some measured factor
    b. Find the correlation between the matched variable and the dependent variable
    c. Randomly assign each member to either the experimental or control group
    d. Both b and c

9. Which is true of the mixed design? (209-210)

    a. The factors are neither within-subjects nor between-subjects
    b. Error variance for the "between comparison" is computed differently from that of the "within comparison"
    c. This design is one of the least used designs despite its practical application because of its degree of difficulty in statistical application
    d. All of the above

10. What is the outcome in a matched design if the participants are matched on a factor that does not correlate with the dependent variable? (212)

    a. Within-group variance will be no smaller than the variance obtained by random assignment alone
    b. Wasted time and effort
    c. Controlled procedures will be required to make an interpretation
    d. Both a and b

11. According to the text, what major way(s) can matching be used? (212-213)

    a. As a control procedure
    b. As a correlation procedure
    c. As an experimental procedure
    d. Both a and c

12. In a within-subjects study that has 4 cells, with 12 subjects in each cell, how many participants are needed? (209-210)

    a. 4
    b. 12
    c. 24
    d. 48

13. When matching on a nominal scale the suggested term is _____. (215)

    a. leveling
    b. stratifying
    c. blocking
    d. intraclass

14. The effects brought about through continued repetition of the tasks are referred to as _____. (207-208)

    a. order effects
    b. intragroup effects
    c. intrasubject effects
    d. repeated block effects

15. Mixed designs assess _____. (209)

    a. main effects of each IV
    b. interactions
    c. a and b
    d. none of the above

Essays

Apply your knowledge of Chapter 9 as you analyze the following questions in detail. Specifically refer to information in the chapter to support your answers.

1. Diagram a between-subjects design and a within-subjects design. Make a chart that defines the major characteristics of these designs. Discuss the statistical differences in analyzing these two designs.

2. Make a table of the advantages and disadvantages of the within-subjects design.

3. Define carryover effect. Give examples of carryover and describe how its effects can be minimized.

4. Discuss different counterbalancing procedures in a detailed step-by-step process.

5. Flowchart a matched-subjects procedure. Give examples of subject characteristics that may be used for matching. Discuss the importance of the correlation between the matching factor and dependent variable in this design.

6. Describe the two main ways (control and experimental) in which the repeated measures design is used in the study of psychological processes. How might a repeated measures factor be used in a mixed design?

7. Discuss matching as a control procedure and matching as an experimental procedure. What are the three main advantages that result from the prior matching of individuals to groups? (Hint: equating, reducing error, identifying interactions) Also explain the differences illustrated by Glass and Stanley between the terms blocking, stratifying, and leveling.

8. Design a matched subjects procedure to examine the effectiveness of behavior therapy versus drug therapy on anorexics that weighed 85 pounds or less. Explain why this strategy would be preferable to a counterbalanced procedure.

RESEARCH ACTIVITIES

The goals of the research activities are to: (1) relate Chapter 9 on an applied learning dimension, and (2) get you involved in research.

1. **Marriage Enrichment Participants: Matching Exercise.** Investigators are interested in the effects of marriage enrichment seminars on married couples in stable relationships. The following couples volunteered to participate in the study. Investigators prescreened the volunteer couples to ensure consistency. In collecting preliminary demographic information from the volunteers it became apparent to the investigators that couples should be matched on the number of years married. This characteristic was highly related to the couple's rating of marriage satisfaction.

   Assignment:
   a. Match the following couples on the number of years married and randomly assign them into Group A, which will receive twelve one-hour marriage enrichment sessions, or Group B, which will meet for twelve one-hour sessions for informal conversation.

   Steps to match participants:

   1. Organize all couples by number of years married by placing them in rank order from highest to lowest.
   2. Pair the couples ranked 1 and 2, 3 and 4, 5 and 6, etc.
   3. Randomly assign couples from each pair to either Group A or Group B.

Couple	Number of Years Married	Rank
A	18	
B	42	
C	1	
D	7	
E	26	
F	39	
G	25	
H	3	
I	12	
J	0	

Random Assignment:

Group A: Marriage Enrichment   **Group B:** Informal Conversation

b. Discuss the advantages and limitations of this design.

2. **Identifying Experimental Designs.**

a. Industrial psychologists were interested in the **effects of goal-setting strategies on work productivity.** Fifty participants participated in this six-month study. All participants were in middle management positions in computer-oriented firms in the Silicon Valley. Participants were randomly assigned. Group 1 received training on goal setting. Participants in Group 1 were asked to keep daily written logs of work goals and checklists of goals accomplished. Supervisors were asked to verify the checklists of goals accomplished on a weekly basis and to present specific personal feedback. Group 2 received no goal-setting training. They met with their supervisors weekly in regularly scheduled general staff meetings and discussed work-related problems. Supervisors were asked to document the work accomplishments of the participant weekly. Work productivity was rated by both the participants and their supervisors at the end of the six-month study.

Questions:
1. Identify the experimental design.
2. What is the independent variable?
3. What is the dependent variable?
4. Diagram this experimental design.
5. What are the potential confounds?

b. Investigators were interested in the role of **maternal touching on the social behavior of chimpanzees.** Chimps were matched by age and then randomly assigned to groups. Group 1 received unlimited maternal touching. Group 2 were raised in complete isolation and received absolutely no maternal touching. Social behavior was measured when chimps were introduced to new social environments with other chimps. Chimps that received no maternal touching displayed significantly greater anti-social behaviors versus those chimps that had received maternal touching. Chimps raised in isolation were self-abusive, and engaged in self-stimulating rocking behaviors.

Questions:
1. Identify the experimental design.
2. What is the independent variable?
3. What is the dependent variable?
4. Diagram this experimental design.
5. What are the potential confounds?

c. Educational psychologists were interested in the impact the **"Just Say No!" program and contracts on drunk driving among teens.** This program was a pilot program. The investigators identified gender as a participant characteristic highly related to alcohol use among teens that would require a matching strategy and analysis statistically. With the cooperation of school officials, 16-year-old students were matched and randomly assigned with equal numbers of males and females in each group. Group A participated in a "Just Say No!" program, which required a one-hour information session instead of P.E. for six weeks. Students were presented with written factual information, motivational lectures, guidance films, and assertiveness training. Students were also encouraged to sign a personal responsibility contract that stipulated that they would not drink and drive. Group B participated in regular P. E. classes for the six-week experimental period. A two-factor factorial analysis was used to analyze for the main effect of the program factor, the main effect of the gender factor, and the interaction.

Questions:
1. Identify the experimental design.
2. What is the independent variable?
3. What is the dependent variable?
4. Diagram this experimental design.
5. What are the potential confounds?

3. **Hyperactive Children and Effective Interventions. Assess carryover. Make treatment order an independent variable:** Another way to deal with carryover is to measure it by making treatment order an independent variable.

Make treatment order an independent variable for a within-subjects design that includes two levels of treatment for participants with attention deficit disorder: (A1) prescription of and (A2) behavior therapy. Subjects' were six-year old boys. Hyperactive behavior was measured over two six-month treatment periods by teachers using a standardized rating scale. Higher scores indicate a greater number of observed hyperactive behaviors.

Graph these findings. What are your conclusions? Is there any evidence of a carryover effect?

	A1(Ritalin)	A2(Behavior Therapy)
Order of Treatment		
B1 (A1- A2)	60	20
B2 (A2 - A1)	20	20

4. **Japanese versus American Students on Math/Science Competence. Mixed Design:** The United States Department of Education has become increasingly concerned over the inferior performance of American children as compared to Japanese children in academic areas such as math and science. As a result, the U.S. federal government has agreed to fund a research project examining the effects of U.S. versus Asian teaching practices on the national standardized test scores of American children in the areas of math and science over a one-month period. You, as the principal investigator, have been asked to develop an experiment using a mixed design to study this issue.

Discuss and diagram the specifics of this study. Specify both the between-subjects factor and within-subjects factor as well as the dependent variables. Discuss possible effects and the interpretation of such effects, provide information regarding statistical analysis, and discuss limitations of the study as well as suggestions for improvement.

5.   **Memory and Music. Repeated measures versus between-subjects design.**
     Compare how many items can be remembered while listening to loud music
     versus silence. Demonstrate the differences between a repeated measures design
     (N=5) and a between-subjects design (N=10). Conduct a repeated measures
     study, and a between-subjects design. Compare the strengths and limitations of
     the two designs. Explore Infotrac to find articles related to music and memory
     and cite these in your discussion.

RESEARCH SUMMARY AND DISCUSSION QUESTIONS

**Extending the Logic of Experimentation: Within Subjects and Matched Subjects
Approaches**

Asch, S. E. (1955). Opinions and social pressure. *Scientific American, 193*, 31-35.

In Chapter 9, Ray defined the within-subject design as an approach that exposes
participants to each treatment condition. This classic study by Asch, which examined the
power of groups on conformity, exemplifies a within-subjects approach.

Participants, along with a group of others, were asked to match the length of a line
compared to other lines and to state their answer aloud. For several trials everyone
picked the correct answer. However, in later trials, group members, who in reality were
confederates, chose the wrong line. In fact, all of the group members preceding the
participant chose the same line incorrectly. Hence, participants were exposed to group
pressure to conform.

Asch found that 75% of all participants went along with the group at least once,
even though they knew it was incorrect. Finally, Asch found that conformity increased as
group size increased (i.e., to seven group members). This within-subject study clearly
demonstrated the power of the group to impact conformity.

Discussion Questions
      1. Describe the experience of participants in each experimental condition.
      2. What are the advantages and disadvantages of this design?

ANSWERS
Fill-in: Self Test
1. Between-subjects design
2. Within-subjects design
3. Error
4. Rejection
5. Internal validity
6. Counterbalance
7. Treatment by order
8. Repeated measures
9. Mixed design
10. Matched-subjects design
11. Matching
12. Randomized block
13. Leveling
14. Fatigue
15. Practice

True/False: Self Test
1. True
2. True
3. True
4. True
5. False
6. True
7. False
8. False
9. True
10. False

Multiple Choice: Self Test
1. A
2. D
3. E
4. C
5. C
6. D
7. B
8. A
9. B
10. D
11. D
12. B
13. C
14. A
15. C

CHAPTER 10

The Ecology of the Experiment:
The Scientist and Subject in Relation to Their Environment

CHAPTER OBJECTIVES: CONCEPT CHECKS

The chapter objectives provide you with a concept checklist. These are things you should know after reading Chapter 10. The accompanying text page numbers are reference aids for your review.

1. Explain the importance of the cultural context in which research takes place. (219)

2. Contrast the perspectives of the scientist, participant, and witness in science. (219)

3. Compare the Leipzig and Paris models. How are these models important to American psychological research? (220-221)

4. Discuss the relationship between the social structure of an experimental situation and the type of information that is generated. (220)

5. Relate the term "ecology" to the research setting. (221)

6. What are experimenter effects? How do they threaten validity? (222)

7. Explain the personal equation in psychological research. (223)

8. Name two measures that are available for assessing the consistency of multiple observers in experimentation? (224)

9. What are examples of experimenter bias? How can experimenter bias be avoided? (223-225)

10. How can subject factors bias an investigation? (230-231)

11. How prevalent are placebo effects? (232)

12. Distinguish between a "blind" study and a "double blind" study. (233-234)

13. How do demand characteristics threaten validity? (234)

14. Why is it important to consider paradigms with respect to the interpretation of research? (236-237)

STUDY GUIDE AND REVIEW

Key Terms

Define each of these terms in your own words. Check your understanding of Chapter 10 by referring to the featured text page.

1. Context (219)

2. Leipzig model (220)

3. Paris model (220)

4. Ecology (221)

5. Ecological validity (222)

6. Experimenter effects (222)

7. Biased data collection (223)

8. Bias (223)

9. Personal equation (223)

10. Cohen's kappa (223)

11. Interrater reliability (223)

12. Experimenter bias (226)

13. Subject factors (230=231)

14. Hawthorne effect (231)

15. Placebo effect (232)

16. Blind study (233)

17. Double blind study (233-234)

18. Demand characteristics (234-235)

19. Quasi-control group (235)

20. Paradigm (237)

Fill-in: Self Test

Fill in the missing word or phrase. Focus your attention on important Chapter 10 details.

1. According to the text, science can be viewed from three separate perspectives: scientist, participant, and _____. (219)

2. An historical model, typified by Wundt's research, makes little differentiation between the participant and the experimenter in terms of the expected roles. This model is called the _____. (220)

3. Danzinger (1959) suggests that American psychological experimentation has been greatly influenced by another historical model, which makes a clear distinction between the roles of scientist and participant. This model is called the _____. (220)

4. _____ refers to the relationship among the scientist, the participants, and the experimental situation in psychological research. (221)

5. An understanding of context and how it relates to the validity of experimental conclusions refers to the concept of _____. (222)

6. The constant error in observation by different scientists is what we call the _____ in psychology. (223)

7. The correlation between two different raters in an observational study is referred to as _____. (223)

8. According to the text, a common statistic for computing an interrater correlation, besides r, is _____. (223)

9. When the experimenter expects something to happen and looks for confirmation of the expectation, this is called a(n) _____. (227)

10. When the person interacting with the participant does not know the hypothesis nor the group she is working with (experimental or control), this is called a _____ study. (233)

11. A participant performs better as a result of being given attention in the experiment. This phenomenon is known as the _____. (231)

12. A treatment with no active agent (e.g., a sugar pill) is called a(n) _____. (232)

13. When a participant's response is influenced by the research setting, this describes
_____. (234)

14. A new government office that oversees research misconduct is called the Office of Research ____. (225)

15. A classic study by Rosenthal and Jacobson (1966) showed the powerful influence of teacher _____ to improve students' IQ scores. (227)

True/False: Self Test

Test your understanding of Chapter 10 by marking the best answer to these true or false items.

1. _____ The witness in science observes the interplay between scientist and participant. (219)

2. _____ History reveals that science has never been completely objective and probably never will be. (219)

3. _____ Scientists never accept limitations. They either control or eliminate them. (220)

4. _____ Some scientists consider the participant-scientist interaction so important that they view all human experimentation as a social event. (220)

5. _____ In the Paris model, the same person could serve as both the experimenter and the participant at different times. (220)

6. _____ Experimenter bias can affect the way data is collected, but it does not influence experimental conclusions. (222-224)

7. _____ Participants in psychological experimentation may react differently to different experimenters. (230-231)

8. _____ The experimenter's expectations of the participant may bias the experimental outcome. (227)

9. _____ Exposing participants to a number of different experimenters and experimental situations is one way to avoid experimenter bias. (228-229)

10. _____ It is incorrect in experimental situations to evaluate participants' perceptions of their treatment simply by asking a few participants how they felt or reacted to your study. (235-236)

<u>**Multiple Choice: Self Test**</u>

Test your Chapter 10 comprehension by circling the best answer to these multiple choice questions.

1. How is validity affected if the scientist-participant interaction is not taken seriously? (219)

    a. Internal validity is seriously threatened
    b. External validity is threatened
    c. Validity is unaffected but reliability is seriously threatened
    d. Both a and b
    e. none of the above

2. This historical model makes a clear distinction concerning the role of the scientist and the participant. What is the name of this model? (220)

    a. Paris
    b. Leipzig
    c. Danzinger
    d. Both a and c

3. Which of the following ideas were proposed by Danzinger? (220)

    a. Psychological research has been influenced by two historical models dating back to the 19th century.
    b. American research has been influenced by a model that suggests scientist and participant are different.
    c. There exists a relationship between the social structure of experimental situations and the type of information that is generated.
    d. All of the above

4. The text refers to the closely interconnected relationship between scientist, participant, and experimental situation as an analogy to _____. (221)

    a. the science of ecology
    b. the science of correlation
    c. intergroup validity
    d. All of the above

5. Which of the following is a type of experimenter effect? (223)

    a. Biased data collection by the experimenter
    b. Experimenter biasing the participant's performance
    c. Interrater reliability
    d. Both a and b

6. This is a common procedure which attempts to minimize biased data collection. (223)

   a. Multiple observers
   b. Ecological validity
   c. Counterbalancing
   d. All of the above

7. How can interrater reliability be evaluated? (223)

   a. Calculation of a correlation between the observation of two observers.
   b. Computation of Cohen's Kappa
   c. Calculation of p-ratio
   d. Both a and b

8. What is the meaning of a higher "r" between the ratings of two independent observers? (223)

   a. The more the ratings represent inconsistent subjective factors of the raters
   b. The less the ratings represent inconsistent subjective factors of the raters
   c. There are significant differences between the two observers
   d. Both b and c

9. What does a low correlation between independent raters suggest? (223)

   a. Few differences between raters
   b. Additional training of raters might be needed
   c. Better operational definitions might be required
   d. Both b and c

10. Research shows that if the experimenter makes an error recording a single piece of data, the error is likely _____. (2223)

   a. supporting the research hypothesis
   b. supporting the null hypothesis
   c. minimized by averaging
   d. Both b and c

11. Which of the following is an example of a way a scientist can change the outcome of an experiment? (225-226)

   a. Deciding to discard a participant's data
   b. Using inappropriate statistical techniques
   c. Performing ad hoc analyses
   d. All of the above

12. One way to control experimenter bias is to _____. (223)

    a. conduct a blind study
    b. include a placebo
    c. assess interrater reliability
    d. measure the Hawthorne effect
    e. All of the above

13. Classes were randomly assigned to teachers. One class was identified as intellectually gifted and the other was identified as intellectually slow; however, in reality, there were no baseline differences between the two classes. Interestingly, after one semester, significant differences were found between the two classes on intelligence. What type of bias would you suspect? (227)

    a. expectancy bias
    b. subject bias
    c. demand characteristics
    d. cultural bias
    e. All of the above

14. According to the text, what is a useful way to eliminate bias from experimentation? (228-230)

    a. View the experiment from varying perspectives
    b. Discard data that are wrong
    c. Alter the experimental design to accommodate participants with special needs
    d. All of the above

15. Upon entering an experimental setting, participants were greeted by a student investigator wearing jeans and a gay pride shirt. Participants were asked to report their feelings about personal freedom, equality, and tolerance. Interestingly, participants in this session reported significantly greater regard for personal freedom, equality, and tolerance than participants in another session where the student investigator wore khaki pants and a polo shirt. These findings may be explained by _____. (234-236)

    a. placebo effect
    b. Hawthorne effect
    c. experimenter bias
    d. expectancy bias
    e. demand characteristics

16. Which of the following is considered a participant factor that potentially confounds experimental interpretation? (230-232)

    a. Participants may be highly motivated to please the experimenter.
    b. Participants may be highly motivated to sabotage the experiment.
    c. Participants may be anxious about participation.
    d. All of the above

17. An experimental situation where neither the participant receiving treatment nor the person giving the treatment knows the treatment administered (e.g., experimental or placebo) is called _____. (233)

    a. single blind
    b. double blind
    c. multiple control groups
    d. Both b and c

18. What are the experimental consequences of demand characteristics and how do they influence experimentation? (234-236)

    a. Demand characteristics can pose a serious threat to internal validity.
    b. Demand characteristics can confound the influence of the independent variable.
    c. Demand characteristics operate under the assumption that the participants accept that they are not being deceived in a deception study.
    d. Both a and b

Essays

Apply your knowledge of Chapter 10 as you analyze the following questions in detail. Specifically refer to information in the chapter to support your answers.

1. Discuss ecology in terms of the interaction of the scientist, the participants, and the context in the experimental process.

2. Explain what Ray meant when he said "experimental results are never just facts."

3. Make a chart illustrating the ways an experimenter can influence the outcome of an experiment. Use the following subheadings: (1) Experimenter Bias, (2) Statistical Decisions, and (3) Interpretation. Address ways to avoid bias and inappropriate decisions in the experimental process.

4. List experimenter characteristics that might influence a participant's behavior in an experimental situation. How should these characteristics be considered when evaluating the experimental design?

5. Discuss the role of the participant as a potential source of bias in experimentation. Make a list of participant factors to consider in the experimental process. Give examples for each and suggest ways to control for these threats to internal validity.

6. Explain the use of multiple observers as it relates to the experimenter bias. Discuss the use of statistics such as Cohen's Kappa in determining interrater reliability. How is a high/low value for Cohen's Kappa interpreted?

7. Describe the placebo effect as well as strategies for controlling this phenomenon.

8. Discuss how a current paradigm influences/biases scientific investigation.

9. Elderly individuals were specially selected to participate in an anti-aging program. All participants had physical and mental examinations, and then were randomly assigned to either the control group or the treatment group. In this blind study, the treatment group took high doses of vitamin C, E, and antioxidants, while the control group took placebo pills. Interestingly, after 6 months, both groups had improved significantly. Explain these findings.

RESEARCH ACTIVITIES

The goals of the research activities are to: (1) relate Chapter 10 on an applied learning dimension, and (2) get you involved in research.

1. **The Volunteer Bias.** Explore InfoTrac to find the work of Rosenthal and Rosnow (1975) on the characteristics of the volunteer participant. In your workbook make a chart of <u>Volunteer Characteristics</u> and <u>Situational Factors</u> that might affect an individual's decision to volunteer for research. Rosenthal and Rosnow listed these characteristics in order of Maximum Confidence and Considerable Confidence.

   a. List the characteristics of individuals who volunteer, according to Rosenthal and Rosnow (1975).
   b. List the situational factors that may affect an individual's decision to volunteer for research participation, according to Rosenthal and Rosnow (1975).
   c. Discuss how you might reduce the volunteer bias.

A. VOLUNTEER CHARACTERISTICS

Maximum Confidence	Considerable Confidence
1.	1.
2.	2.
3.	3.
4.	4.
5.	5.

B. SITUATIONAL FACTORS

Maximum Confidence   Considerable Confidence

1.   1.
2.   2.
3.   3.
4.   4.
5.   5.

2. **Content Analysis of Violence on Network News.** Work with a partner and observe news programs for one week. Decide on particular news programs, observation dates, and times.

   a. Find at least three journal articles using InfoTrac related to this topic. List the articles in your workbook following APA guidelines.

   b. Operationally define violence so that you and your partner will be able to accurately observe and measure it when viewing a news program. Write your operational definition in your workbook.

   c. Design a coding sheet in your workbook. Include the date, the news program, and the categories you used to tally your observations of violence. You may also wish to include context information like whom the violence was against: men, women, children, animals, nature, etc. Further, you may wish to record the media's ethnic representation of who perpetrates violence.

   d. Observe and collect data. Calculate means and standard deviations.

   e. Discuss any problems incurred in this investigation.

3. **Calculate Interrater Reliability.**   Using the data from the content analysis of sexism on commercials during TV talk shows, calculate the interrater reliability between the observations of you and your colleague. Your instructor will advise you on his/her preferred method of calculating interrater reliability. Two commonly used statistics for determining interrater reliability are the Pearson's Product Moment Correlation Coefficient (r), and Cohen's Kappa (Bakeman & Gottman, 1989). According to Bakeman and Gottman (1989) a calculated .70 relationship or greater is an acceptable index of interrater reliability. Calculate interrater reliability and show your work. How does your calculated r compare to the recommendations of Bakeman and Gottman?

4. **Obesity, Weight Loss and Experimenter Effects.** Recognizing that many of her middle-aged male patients were overweight, a physician decided that she would attempt to determine the most effective method for facilitating weight loss in her clients. After making a list of all of her overweight clients, she selected 10 men for each of the following three groups based on their personality characteristics and her belief that they would be more likely to adhere to a specific condition. Group 1 would be given a 3 week supply of appetite suppressants. Group 2 would be given a list of the specific meals, snacks, and fluids that they should consume each day over the following 3 week period, Group 3 would be given a placebo pill that looked and tasted precisely like the appetite suppressant given to Group 1. In regards to Groups 1 and 2, whom she considered to possess great self-discipline and internal motivation, she met with those patients every day for 15 minutes each and lavished considerable praise on them for any weight loss demonstrated. Due to the fact that she reserved Group 3 for patients she believed to possess little self-discipline or desire to lose the excess weight, the daily meetings entailed a weigh in and a self-recording of their weight on a chart. At the end of the three week period, results revealed that groups 1 and 2 lost an average of 6.5 and 6.2 pounds, respectively. Group 3 lost an average of 1.5 pounds over this time period.

Discuss the possible explanations for these findings. Identify the limitations/confounds of the study. Redesign the study to control for or eliminate the problems identified.

5. **Cultural and Social Bias.** Which of the following are universal across all cultures? Define these constructs within your culture. Compare how these constructs are defined in other cultures using InfoTrac.

   a. Time

   b. Change

   c. Independence

   d. Feminism

   e. Stress

   f. Success

RESEARCH SUMMARY AND DISCUSSION QUESTIONS

The Ecology of the Experiment: The Scientist and Research Participant in Relation to their Environments

Rosenthal, R., & Jacobson, L. (1966). Teachers' expectancies: Determinates of pupils' IQ gains. *Psychological Reports, 19*, 115-118.

      In Chapter 10, Ray discussed the effect of bias on experimentation. Rosenthal and Jacobsen's study illustrates the power of bias on experimental outcomes.

      Teachers' expectations of students were manipulated in this study. Teachers were told that certain students were academically gifted and others were not, when in fact, students were randomly assigned into these categories. There were no significant differences between students who were identified as intellectually gifted and students who were not. However, after a year, students identified as gifted showed significantly greater IQ scores than the comparison group of students. These results showed that participants were strongly influenced by biased expectations. Moreover, biased expectations became a self-fulfilling prophecy.

Discussion Questions
1. Discuss the type of biased teacher/student interactions that likely occurred in this study.
2. Discuss participants' sensitivity to subtle cues in experimentation.

SUGGESTED READINGS

Rosenthal, R., & Rosnow, R.L. (1975). *The volunteer subject*. New York: John Wiley & Sons.

ANSWERS
Fill-in: Self Test
1. Witness
2. Leipzig model
3. Paris model
4. Ecology
5. Ecological validity
6. Personal equation
7. Interrater reliability
8. Cohen's Kappa
9. Self-fulfilling prophecy
10. Blind
11. Hawthorne effect
12. Placebo
13. Demand characteristics
14. Integrity
15. Expectations

True/False: Self Test
1. True
2. True
3. False
4. True
5. False
6. False
7. True
8. True
9. True
10. False

Multiple Choice: Self Test
1. C
2. A
3. D
4. A
5. D
6. A
7. D
8. B
9. D
10. A
11. D
12. C
13. A
14. A
15. E
16. D
17. B
18. D

CHAPTER 11

Quasi-Experimental, Correlational, and Naturalistic Observational Designs

CHAPTER OBJECTIVES: CONCEPT CHECKS

The chapter objectives provide you with a concept checklist. These are things you should know after reading Chapter 11. The accompanying text page numbers are reference aids for your review.

1. How is the balance between internal and external validity affected by the experimental design? (243)

2. Distinguish between closed and open systems in experimentation. (242-424)

3. How is control related to ruling out alternative explanations and rival hypotheses? (243)

4. Is internal or external validity more important in good research? (243)

5. What is archival research and when is it used? (245)

6. How do some quasi-experimental designs combine naturalistic observation with more experimental-like procedures in real-life situations? (251)

7. Give examples of four non-retrospective quasi-experimental time series designs and list their defining characteristics. (252)

8. When are retrospective studies most commonly used? (261-262)

9. What is the objective of the correlational procedure? How is it limited? (262-264)

10. List two potential problems with respect to naturalistic observation. (264-270)

STUDY GUIDE AND REVIEW

Key Terms

Define each of these terms in your own words. Check your understanding of Chapter 11 by referring to the featured text page.

1. Quasi-experimental design (242)

2. Internal validity (243)

3. External validity (243)

4. Closed system (242)

5. Open system (243)

6. Retrospective (245, 261-262)

7. Archival research (245)

8. Correlational designs (252)

9. Naturalistic observation (252)

10. Time series design (252)

11. Interrupted time series design (253)

12. Multiple time series design (256)

13. Nonequivalent before-after design (258-259)

14. Ex post facto designs (261-262)

15. Correlational procedures (262)

16. Third-variable problem (264)

17. Reactive behavior (266)

18. Unobtrusive observations (266)

19. Selective perception (267)

20. Concealed identity (268-269)

21. Participant observation (269)

Fill-in: Self Test

Fill in the missing word or phrase. Focus your attention on important Chapter 11 details.

1. For a given situation, the task of the research _____ is to help support inferences of the greatest strength possible. (242)

2. Throughout the history of science, the prime objective of the research situation has been experimental _____. (242)

3. An experiment in which the important factors that influence the environment are controlled by the experimenter is called a(n) _____ system. (242)

4. High-control designs help rule out alternative explanations and rival hypotheses and therefore ensure a greater degree of _____ validity. (243)

5. The world outside the lab, where subjects are being influenced by a number of uncontrollable factors, describes a(n) _____ system. (243)

6. The generalizability of an experimental outcome is referred to as its _____. (243)

7. Utilizing existing records in research, which were collected before the time of the study though not for purposes of the study, illustrates _____. (245)

8. A research alternative that combines naturalistic observation with more experimental-like procedures in real-life situations describes types of _____. (251)

9. A design that attempts to describe the relationship that exists between two variables is called _____. (252)

10. Although a researcher may use correlational designs for confirming predictions, they do not allow one to infer _____. (252)

11. An interrupted time series design, which attempts to rule out alternative interpretations by including a control group, is called the _____. (256)

12. When a participant's behavior is influenced by the presence of the observer, this illustrates _____ behavior. (266)

13. An attempt to use empirical procedures for studying relationships between events that have occurred in the past characterizes _____ designs. (261)

14. When observations are markedly influenced by what we expect to see, this describes _____, which may greatly impact the accuracy of our observations. (267)

True/False: Self Test

Test your understanding of Chapter 11 by marking the best answer to these true or false items.

1. _____ In quasi-experimental, correlational, and naturalistic designs the researcher accepts that there are uncontrollable factors that influence the experimental outcome. (243)

2. _____ Moving a study to the field eliminates one's ability to use tight experimental control to manipulate variables. (243)

3. _____ B. F. Skinner's use of a Skinner box, and the manner in which he fed and cared for his animal subjects, exemplified open system experimentation. (243)

4. _____ It is equally important to have external validity as well as internal validity in the experimental process. (243)

5. _____ Naturally occurring phenomena (e.g., the 1992 riots in Los Angeles following the Rodney King verdict) defy true experimental control. (245-246)

6. _____ In most cases, the internal validity of our research is decreased as we move from the laboratory to more natural settings. (247)

7. _____ If variables are not correlated, then it is important to employ a more controlled research setting to establish a causal link. (252)

8. _____ A multiple time series design is a within-subjects design like the interrupted-time series; however, it attempts to rule out alternative interpretations by including a control group. (256)

9. _____ Retrospective and ex post facto designs produce weak forms of inference. (261)

10. _____ Reactive behavior portrays what people are like when they know they are being observed; it tells us nothing about behavior under normal circumstances. (266)

Multiple Choice: Self Test

Test your Chapter 11 comprehension by circling the best answer to these multiple choice questions.

1. Which procedure(s) is/are commonly used in research conducted outside the laboratory? (243)

    a. Quasi-experimental
    b. Correlational
    c. Naturalistic
    d. All of the above

2. Weighing whether one would want to give up rigorous experimental controls in order to better study real-world problems addresses what issue? (243)

    a. Research using correlational vs. quasi-experimental designs
    b. The balance of internal and external validity
    c. Applied vs. theoretical research
    d. All of the above

3. In Bandura's (1970) classic Bobo doll experiment, aggressive modeling was carefully manipulated in the laboratory to examine how it affected children's behavior. The tightly controlled nature of this research design exemplifies _____ validity.   (243)

    a. internal
    b. external
    c. face
    d. interaction
    e. Both b and d

4. Which of the following is true of quasi-experimental designs? (251)

    a. They are referred to as evaluation research designs because they are used to evaluate the impact of some variable on an ongoing process
    b. They are extremely useful in uncovering potential relationships with complex psychological phenomena in a variety of settings
    c. The designs are useful in showing when a relationship does not exist and reduce the need for performing highly controlled designs
    d. All of the above

5. A within-subjects design that utilizes the performance of a single group of participants who are measured once before and once after the experimental treatment describes the _____. (253)

    a. single group, pretest-posttest design

    b. interrupted time series design
    c. nonequivalent time series design
    d. multiple time series design

6. One way to overcome the weakness of the single-group pretest-posttest design is to utilize a design that involves several pretest and several post-test measurements. This design is called a_____. (253)

    a. multiple-group, pretest-posttest design
    b. interrupted time series
    c. nonequivalent time series
    d. multiple time series design

7. This schematic diagram of a widely used design in educational research illustrates the _____. (258)

Group	Pretest	Treatment	Posttest	D
Experimental	01	X	02	01-02
Control	01		02	01-02

    a. interrupted time series design
    b. ABAD design
    c. multiple time series design
    d. nonequivalent before-after design

8. What is an advantage of the nonequivalent before-after design? (259-260)

    a. It is practical for small samples.
    b. Many threats to internal validity such as history are ruled out by this design.
    c. Selection-maturation is controlled and does not threaten internal validity.
    d. All of the above

9. Which of the following is a quasi-experimental design? (252-260)

    a. time-series
    b. interrupted time-series
    c. multiple time-series
    d. nonequivalent time-series
    e. All of the above

10. The work of Darwin, Lorenz, and Tinbergen are classic examples of what experimental technique? (264-270)

    a. qualitative research
    b. correlational research
    c. naturalistic observation
    d. quasi-experimental design

11. Which of the following is true of the correlational procedure? (262-263)

    a. Correlation does not imply a particular statistic.
    b. There are no independent or dependent variables.
    c. Correlational procedures are an important initial step of the inferential process.
    d. All of the above

12. Which of the following is true of correlation? (262-263)

    a. Correlational results must be interpreted in correlational terms.
    b. A lack of correlation does not rule out the possibility of causality if a more intensive experimental design is utilized.
    c. A lack of correlation rules out any possibility of causality.
    d. Both a and c

13. According to the text, what is an advantage of the naturalistic design? (264-269)

    a. It is very primitive in its method, yet it is the greatest single application of a scientific research technique.
    b. It has a high degree of internal validity.
    c. It is an important first step in describing the relationships of naturally occurring variables and studying these processes as they unfold over time.
    d. It tends to rely heavily on objective data and selective perception.

Essays

Apply your knowledge of Chapter 11 as you analyze the following questions in detail. Specifically refer to information in the chapter to support your answers.

1. What are the advantages and limitations of the quasi-experimental design in comparison to the "true" experimental design?

2. Why do you think there is growing concern for the application of research findings and how does this influence contemporary research?

3. Examine problems that may be associated with retrospective research. Address the participant's memory and social desirability. Further address the problem of response verification.

4. Discuss how correlational research is useful in disconfirming potential causal relationships.

5. What are the advantages and disadvantages of becoming a participant in naturalistic studies?

6. Describe the relationship between internal and external validity in research. Relate your response to the concept of closed and open systems and explain the advantages and disadvantages of each. Give examples of situations in which it is possible to perform useful research in situations of diminished control.

7. Discuss the two functions of naturalistic observation. Describe the limitations of this method as well as strategies for counteracting these limitations. Also include a discussion of the strengths and weaknesses of naturalistic observation as a research method.

8. Detail the kind of quasi-experimental design that you would use if you wanted to compare the anti-social attitudes of adolescents who had been highly exposed to violent media compared to those who had been minimally exposed to violent media.

9. Describe how unexpected event like the attack on the World Trade Center can be scientifically studied. What are the critical issues to consider when you conduct research on the psychological effect of unexpected tragedies or disasters?

10. What are the limitations of studying the effects of disasters (ex. the Thai tsunami) that unexpectedly occur?

RESEARCH ACTIVITIES

The goals of the research activities are to: (1) relate Chapter 11 on an applied learning dimension, and (2) get you involved in research.

1. **Gender and Helping Behavior. A Quasi-experimental Study.** Your objective is to measure the degree of helping behavior on your campus. Approach 10 females and 10 males who are present around the student union area of your campus. Ask participants if they could help you by giving you change for a dollar to make an important phone call. Record their gender, and the degree to which they were willing to be helpful on a 5 point scale (i.e., where a 1= not at all helpful, and a 5 = very helpful). You may also wish to record other types of demographic information (e.g., age, ethnicity) or to systematically manipulate variables (e.g., the way you are dressed).

   a. Operationally define the behavior you will record.

   b. Flow chart your planned procedure in your workbook.

c. Create a frequency tally coding sheet in your workbook for observation.

d. Record data using your workbook coding sheet.

e. Summarize your data by calculating frequency totals and converting to percentages.

f. Interpret the data and describe any observed patterns of behavior.

g. Discuss the limitations of your study.

h. Discuss recommendations for improving this study.

i. Research related studies and list three references.

j. Write an abstract for this study in APA format. Be prepared to discuss your findings in class.

2. **Happiness, Financial Wealth, and Marital Status. A Correlational Study.**
Research Diener's work on happiness (i.e., subjective well-being). Using the forms on the next page, collect data from twenty participants, asking them to (1) rate their general degree of happiness, (2) approximate their yearly gross income, and (3) indicate their marital status. Calculate three Pearson's product moment correlation coefficients to describe the relationships between these three variables. Interpret your results. Are your findings consistent with other studies in this area? Discuss the limitations of this study.

CONSENT

I am a student in a college-level experimental research methods course. I am learning how to conduct experiments and how to analyze data. I would appreciate a few minutes of your time to respond to the following questions about general happiness. These questions are not of a sensitive nature, but if you are in any way uncomfortable, you are free to stop at any time. Your honest response is greatly appreciated. Your answers are strictly anonymous. The information from this study will be used for educational purposes only. If you have any questions, I will be happy to answer them. Thank you for participating.

Happiness Survey

1. Circle your degree of general happiness on the following scale.

    1   2   3   4   5   6   7

    Unhappy   Happy

    Comments:

2. Circle your approximate yearly gross income.

    1. 0 to $5,000
    2. $5,001 to $10,000
    3. $10,001 to $15,000
    4. $15,001 to $20,000
    5. $20,001 to $25,000
    6. $25,001 to $30,000
    7. $30,001 to $35,000
    8. $35,001 to $40,000
    9. $40,001 to $45,000
    10. $45,001 to $50,000
    11. Above $50,000

3. What is your marital status?

    1. single, not currently in a long term relationship
    2. single, currently in a long term relationship
    3. married (not divorced or separated)

PEARSON'S CORRELATION COEFFICIENT CALCULATIONS:

FILL IN THE MISSING CORRELATION INFORMATION:

	Happiness	Financial Status	Marital Status
Happiness	1.00		
Financial Status		1.00	
Marital Status			1.00

RESEARCH FINDINGS:

3. **Effect of Three Strikes Law on Crime. Design an Interrupted Time Series Study.** You are a forensic psychologist interested in the effect of new California legislation entitled "Three Strikes and You're Out" on the frequency of violent crime in the state. Basically this law proposes that each time someone is convicted and put in jail for a violent crime, this constitutes a strike. Three such convictions result in life imprisonment or the death penalty. Design an interrupted time series study that will assess the effectiveness of this law. Discuss the limitations of this design and how such limitations affect the interpretation of results.

4. Use Infotrac to find three scientific studies related to the 9/11 attack on the World Trade Center. Identify if the studies are correlational, quasi-experimental, or naturalistic observations.

5. Design a correlational, quasi-experimental or naturalistic study that examines the relationship between students' blog activity and academic achievement. Identify the key components of your research design. Use Infotrac to find related articles.

RESEARCH SUMMARY AND DISCUSSION QUESTIONS

Quasi-experimental, Correlational and Naturalistic Observational Designs

Zajonc, R. B., & Markus, G. B. (1975). Birth order and intellectual development. *Psychological Review, 82,* 74-88.

      In this quasi-experimental study, Zajonc and Markus used archival data to examine the relationship between birth order and intellectual development. According to Ray, in Chapter 11, a quasi-experimental study does not involve random assignment into experimental groups. Because birth order could not be randomly assigned, Zajonc and Markus chose a quasi-experimental design. They found that intellectual ability decreased steadily from the first-born to fifth-born child, and as family size increased intellectual ability decreased. The investigators also found that first-borns tended to be more intellectual than later borns; however, compared to later borns, first-borns tended to be more anxious and neurotic. Later-borns, on the other hand, tended to be more social and affectionate, and youngest children tended to be more happy and creative.

      Compared to true experimental designs, the findings in a quasi-experimental design are more limited. Thus, caution must exercised by the investigators when interpreting results. Causal conclusions are not appropriate in studies that use a quasi-experimental approach. Therefore, one may not conclude from the aforementioned study that birth order caused one to be more or less intelligent.

Discussion Questions
1.   What kind of quasi-experimental design was illustrated in Zajonc and Markus' study?
2.   Discuss the limitations of this design?

SUGGESTED READINGS

Diener, E., Horowitz, J., & Emmons, R. A. (1985). Happiness of the very wealthy. *Social Indicators Research, 16,* 157-168.

    Interesting information especially for those who are seeking to attain happiness via external sources.

Festinger, L., Riecken, H.W., & Schacter, S. (1982). When prophecy fails. In A. Pines & C. Maslach (Eds.), *Experiencing social psychology: Readings and projects (2nd ed.)* (pp.69-75). New York: Knopf.

This is a classic example of a participant study on people who predict the end of the world. The investigators convinced the members that they were also true believers but concealed their interest in studying the group's behavior. The investigator continued to observe the groups even when their catastrophic predictions failed. Interestingly, the members became more committed to their beliefs after their prophecy failed. They believed their spiritual actions had saved the world from catastrophe.

ANSWERS

Fill-in: Self Test
1. Design
2. Control
3. Closed
4. Internal
5. Open
6. External validity
7. Archival research
8. Quasi-experimental designs
9. Correlational
10. Causation
11. Multiple time series design
12. Reactive
13. Retrospective or ex post facto
14. Selective perception

True/False: Self Test

1. True
2. False
3. False
4. True
5. True
6. True
7. False
8. False
9. True
10. True

Multiple Choice: Self Test

1. D
2. B
3. A
4. D
5. A
6. B
7. D
8. B
9. E
10. C
11. D
12. D
13. C

CHAPTER 12

Single Subject Designs

CHAPTER OBJECTIVES: CONCEPT CHECKS

The chapter objectives provide you with a concept checklist. These are things you should know after reading Chapter 12. The accompanying text page numbers are reference aids for your review.

1.   What is the history of the single-subject design? (274-275)

2.   How are the objectives of the case study design and the experimental single-subject design different? (274, 277-281)

3.   Describe the importance of context in the naturalistic case study. (278)

4.   In the one-shot case study design, what does the "one-shot" refer to? (279-281)

5.   What are the advantages of the case study design? In your judgment, where in psychology would it be especially useful? (278-279)

6.   Discuss the strength of inferences with respect to the case study design. (278)

7.   What is the importance of baseline measurement in the experimental single-subject approach? (281)

8.   When there is more than one participant, how is data dealt with differently in the single-subject design versus traditional designs? (274)

9.   Describe the reversal design, the multiple baseline design, and the multielement design in terms of their defining features, advantages, and limitations. (281-289)

10. What are some of the recent trends in single-subject research? (289-290)

STUDY GUIDE AND REVIEW

Key Terms

Define each of these terms in your own words. Check your understanding of Chapter 12 by referring to the featured text page.

1. Single-subject design (274-275)

2. Case study (264-269)

3. One-shot case study (278-281)

4. Experimental single-subject designs (281-282)

5. Time series approach (281)

6. Baseline (281)

7. Intrasubject replication (282)

8. Intersubject replication (282)

9. Reversal design (2282)

10. ABA design (283)

11. ABAB design (283)

12. Multiple baseline design (286)

13. Multielement designs (288)

14. Carryover problem (288)

15. Order effects (288)

16. Counterbalancing (288)

Fill-in: Self Test

Fill in the missing word or phrase. Focus your attention on important Chapter 12 details.

1. Single-subject approaches do not require _____ statistics. (274)

2. _____ designs offer a powerful method for determining which technique works best with a given individual. (274)

3. A(n) _____ is a narrative description of an individual or some aspect of an individual that brings together the person's history and present situation. (278)

4. The value of the naturalistic case study is that it is possible to describe the individual case in its actual _____. (278)

5. Although less powerful, one could use the one-shot case study in a(n) _____ manner to study the effects of an event that took place in the past. (279)

6. Single-subject designs are not based on the same methodological considerations as traditional experiments; therefore gaining _____ over extraneous variables requires a different type of methodology. (281)

7. The logic of the _____ approach is to establish a series of measurements over time. (281)

8. The more stable the _____ measurement sequence, the easier it is to establish that the independent variable has influenced the dependent variable. (281)

9. As with other research methods, it is important that the dependent variable be clearly described through _____. (282)

10. The ABAB single-subject design, which relies primarily on logic to gain its degree of experimental control is a type of _____ design. (283)

11. A limitation of the multiple baseline design is that each behavior being monitored must be relatively _____ of the other. (286)

12. A(n) _____ design compares the different levels of a given treatment variable or different treatments. It is also referred to as the alternating treatment design. (288)

13. The key feature of the multielement design is that it incorporates many _____, which may be fast paced. (288)

14. Replication is a tool that allows the investigator to reproduce the same relationships a number of times. This supports the contention that the relationship is _____. (288)

15. Rearranging the order of treatments to control for carryover is called _____. (288)

True/False: Self Test

Test your understanding of Chapter 12 by marking the best answer to these true or false items.

1. _____ Single-subject designs do not consider issues of internal and external validity. (274)

2. _____ One hallmark of Skinner's experimental analysis of behavior was that data from a single participant remained separate and were not statistically averaged with data from other participants. (275)

3. _____ Single-subject designs have had a consistent reputation of being the most rigorous scientific method with the highest degree of control. (275-276)

4. _____ In the single-subject design, descriptive and experimental intents may be combined. (276)

5. _____ Unlike other designs, the goal of single-subject design is simply to understand behavioral patterns, not to eliminate rival hypotheses. (276)

6. _____ In clinical psychology, one of the most highly used methods for studying individual participants is the naturalistic case study. (278)

7. _____ As an experimental design, the one-shot case study gives us the ability to make strong inferences. (279-281)

8. _____ At times the single-subject design may be used with a larger number of participants. (281)

9. _____ An advantage of the experimental single-subject design is that extraneous variables can be completely ruled out. (281)

10. _____ Unlike the reversal designs, which work only for behaviors that are readily reversible, multiple baseline designs can be used for behaviors that are permanently changed by the experimental treatment. (281, 282-284)

Multiple Choice: Self Test

Test your Chapter 12 comprehension by circling the best answer to these multiple choice questions.

1. Which is true of the single-subject design? (2274-275)

    a. Control and clear operational definitions are critical in establishing a relationship between independent and dependent variables.
    b. Results involve averaging and establishing group means.
    c. Sampling of participants is important in controlling error.
    d. All of the above

2. Which famous psychologist used a methodology that came to be known as the experimental analysis of behavior? (275)

    a. Pavlov
    b. Wundt
    c. Skinner
    d. Freud

3. In the 1920's, psychology began to shift to larger sample sizes and the use of statistical evaluation. This was due to the work of _____. (275)

    a. Skinner
    b. Fisher
    c. Pavlov
    d. Pearson

4. What is the defining purpose of the single-subject design? (277)

    a. The purpose is primarily descriptive and is represented by the case study.
    b. Single-subject designs are experimental in their intent to focus on the impact of the independent variable on the dependent variable.
    c. Single-subject designs are primarily for questions that require assessment of behavior with limited time and control.
    d. Both a and b

5. Much of the information that we now know about dissociative identity disorder has been gained from what kind of study? (278)

    a. Qualitative design
    b. Quasi-experimental design
    c. Naturalistic case study design
    d. Personality inventory design

6. The case study design that summarizes an experimenter's direct observation of a participant's behavior after some sort of treatment has been administered is called the _____. (279)

    a. systematic case study
    b. one-shot case study
    c. baseline case study
    d. All of the above

7. In a single-subject schematic diagram that uses the symbols "X" and "O," the "O" represents _____. (279)

    a. the control group
    b. the reversal
    c. the observation
    d. the treatment

8. How can the case study be a useful tool in research? (278)

    a. The observation may suggest new hypotheses.
    b. The study may demonstrate rare phenomena.
    c. The study may show exceptions to established rules.
    d. All of the above

9. Establishing a _____ is extremely important in a time series design because it serves as a reference point with which to compare changes associated with the introduction of the independent variable. (281)

    a. group mean
    b. blind observer
    c. baseline
    d. treatment

10. This type of replication is specific to the single-subject design and refers to the use of more than one participant to improve generalizability. (282)

    a. Intrasubject replication
    b. Intersubject replication
    c. Systematic replication
    d. External replication

11. Reliability in single subject designs is established using _____. (282)

    a. statistics
    b. more participants
    c. intrasubject replication
    d. intersubject replication
    e. All of the above

12. Causality in experimental single subject designs _____. (283)

    a. is not possible because the single subject design is descriptive only
    b. is only possible if replicated using additional participants
    c. is possible if participants are randomly assigned to treatment conditions
    d. is supported by reversal designs and intrasubject replication
    e. is not possible because independent variables are not manipulated

13. In a single-subject design, when the baseline and treatment conditions are shifted and repeated, this is called _____. (282-283)

    a. repeated within measures
    b. reversal
    c. stability criterion
    d. intersubject shift

14. According to the text, what specifically does the ABA design represent in terms of observations? (283)

    a. Observation before, during, and after the treatment condition
    b. Observation of many reversals
    c. Observation of multiple baseline measures
    d. All of the above

15. What is a limitation of the reversal design? (285)

    a. You may not treat a group as if it were a single subject.
    b. You may not use multiple reversals.
    c. One cannot determine the effect of introducing the treatment.
    d. It will work only when we are studying the effect of treatments on behaviors that quickly return to baseline levels when the treatments are over.

16. Which design monitors several behaviors of a single participant simultaneously and then applies treatment to one of these behaviors at a time once baseline levels are established? (286)

   a. Reversal design
   b. One-shot design
   c. Multiple baseline
   d. Multielement design

Essays

Apply your knowledge of Chapter 12 as you analyze the following questions in detail. Specifically refer to information in the chapter to support your answers.

1. Create an outline that addresses the defining features of the single-subject designs described in the text. Address the strengths and weaknesses of each of these designs.

2. Defend the single-subject design as a rigorous experimental process. Address the criticisms of this design.

3. Flowchart and compare the features of the single-subject case study design and the single-subject experimental design.

4. Discuss the benefits and limitations of using a single-subject design versus an experimental design in which group means or averages are calculated. What types of questions would these different designs allow/not allow you to answer? Describe the differences in the goals of each method.

5. Describe both the strengths and weaknesses of the following experimental single-subject designs: reversal design, multiple-baseline design, and multielement design. Discuss strategies that would counteract the limitations cited.

6. In interpreting the results of single-subject experimental designs, what type of evidence/tools would be useful in demonstrating that the treatment influenced the dependent variable or that the relationship between two variables was stable? In addition, describe how the interpretation of findings from single-subject experimental designs differs from the interpretation of traditional experimental designs.

7. Explain the concepts of intrasubject replication and intersubject replication in the single-subject design. How do these terms relate to internal and external validity?

8. Give an example of several treatment conditions that would permanently affect the participant so that behavior would be irreversible; thus, making an ABA design inappropriate.

9. In your own words, what is Meehl's point related to significance testing?

10. In science is it always necessary to use statistics to analyze data. Explain why or why not you agree with this statement.

RESEARCH ACTIVITIES

The goals of the research activities are to: (1) relate Chapter 12 on an applied learning dimension, and (2) get you involved in research.

1. **Multiple Baseline Studies.**

   A. **Systematic Desensitization of Multiple Phobias.** In order to treat a woman suffering from several phobias which include a fear of dogs, flying, and receiving injections, a clinical psychologist wishes to use systematic desensitization treatment in which the patient will be directly and gradually exposed to the very objects which she fears. To assess treatment outcome, the dependent variable measured will be self-reported ratings of anxiety. Design the study using a multiple-baseline design, graph possible results of a successful intervention, and provide interpretation of the results discussed. Describe any limitations of your study and provide suggestions for improvement that could be incorporated into a follow-up study.

   B. **Self Abusive Behavior of an Autistic Child.** You are a clinician attempting to reduce self-abusive behavior in a 5-year old autistic boy. The child exhibits self-abusive behavior both at home and in his special day classes. Thus, the behavior occurs across two settings. Consider interventions that may effectively reduce the self-abusive behaviors of this child. Design a single subject multiple baseline design (across situations-home and school). Graph a rough sketch of the results you expect after employing your intervention.

2. **Reversal Design.**

   Reinforcement of Prosocial Behavior in Preschool Child. This applied single-subject study was interested in the effect of positive reinforcement on the prosocial behavior of a typical four-year-old child.

Prosocial Criteria as Established by the Parent and Child:

Helps parent with dinner
Plays with the baby
Answers phone politely
Reads book to brother
Feeds cat

Positive Reinforcement as Established by the Parent and Child:

1. The child will make a chart listing the prosocial criteria and post the chart.
2. The child will mark a star each time she accomplishes a prosocial behavior. The child will also notify the parent of each behavior.
3. The child and parent will total the stars at the end of the week.
4. The parent will reward the child $1.00 for every 10 stars.
5. The parent will take the child to the store to spend the reward.

Week 1: The following prosocial behavior is recorded during the baseline phase. (A)

Sunday
Monday   X
Tuesday   XX
Wednesday   X
Thursday
Friday   X
Saturday   X

Week 2: The following prosocial behavior is recorded during the treatment (reinforcement) phase. (B)

Sunday   XXXX
Monday   XXXXX
Tuesday   XXXX
Wednesday   XXXXX
Thursday   XXXX
Friday   XXXXXXX
Saturday   XXXXXX

Week 3: The following prosocial behavior is recorded during reversal back to baseline (no reinforcement) conditions. (A)

Sunday   XXX
Monday   XX
Tuesday   X
Wednesday   X
Thursday
Friday
Saturday

Week 4: The following prosocial behavior is recorded during intrasubject replication of the treatment (reinforcement) phase. (B)

Sunday	XXXX
Monday	XXXXX
Tuesday	XXXXX
Wednesday	XXX
Thursday	XXX
Friday	XXXXXX
Saturday	XXXXXX

Assignment: Graph these data and report your conclusions.

INTERSUBJECT REPLICATION: The study continued in an attempt to demonstrate intersubject replication with a younger child, two years old, in the same family. Utilizing the same criteria, the following data were collected.

Week 1: The following prosocial behavior is recorded during the baseline (no reinforcement) phase. (A)

Sunday	
Monday	X
Tuesday	X
Wednesday	X
Thursday	
Friday	X
Saturday	X

Week 2: The following prosocial behavior is recorded during the treatment (reinforcement) phase. (B)

Sunday	
Monday	X
Tuesday	
Wednesday	X
Thursday	X
Friday	X
Saturday	XX

Week 3: The following prosocial behavior is recorded during reversal back to baseline (no reinforcement) conditions. (A)

Sunday	
Monday	X
Tuesday	X
Wednesday	X
Thursday	
Friday	X
Saturday	X

Week 4: The following prosocial behavior is recorded during intrasubject replication of the treatment (reinforcement) phase. (B)

Sunday	
Monday	
Tuesday	X
Wednesday	X
Thursday	
Friday	X
Saturday	XX

Assignment: Graph these data and report your conclusions. Finally, what articles can you locate in the research journals that relate to this case study?

REFERENCES: Using InfoTrac find three journal articles that relate to this study. Organize your references in APA format.

3. **Case Study: Study Your Dreams -- Journal.** For one week organize time every morning before you get out of bed to record your dreams in your workbook. Before you retire, place your workbook and a pen by your bed. Create a mind set by repeating to yourself, "I will remember my dreams tonight." Immediately when you awaken in the morning, write down your dream(s) in detail. Consider the following information:

a. Who was in your dream? How many family members? How many friends or colleagues? How many strangers? How many males? How many females?

b. Where did your dream take place and what was the setting? Inside or outside?

c. What was the theme of your dream? Conflict? Happiness? Anger? Aggression? Intimacy? Calamity?

<u>**DREAM JOURNAL**</u>

DAY 1

DAY 2

DAY 3

DAY 4

DAY 5

DAY 6

DAY 7

Assignment: In your workbook organize a case study report. Discuss any patterns that you have observed from your journal entries. Research this topic using InfoTrac. Cite at least three references, using APA format to support your research findings.

<u>CASE STUDY REPORT</u>

<u>REFERENCES (3 minimum in APA format)</u>

4. **Skinner's Nobel Prize in Science**
   Use InfoTrac to find B.F Skinner's single subject research that led to the Noble prize. What was ground breaking about this research?

5. **Applied Behavior Analysis**
   Use InfoTrac to explore Applied Behavior Analysis research with autistic children. Find a research article on this subject that used a single subject design. Identify the question, describe the design, and explain the outcome. Comment on the strengths and weaknesses of this design.

RESEARCH SUMMARY AND DISCUSSION QUESTIONS

Single-Subject Designs

Dement, W. (1960). The effect of dream deprivation. *Science, 131,* 1705-1707.

This study on sleep deprivation by Dement is an example of a single subject design ABAB design, although, as explained by Ray in Chapter 12, more than one participant was used in this study.

First, participants' baseline sleep patterns were established (phase A). Next, participants were deprived of REM dream sleep (phase B). Following several nights of deprivation, participants were allowed to recover and sleep without interruption (phase A). Lastly, participants were again deprived of sleep (phase B).

Dement found that loss of REM dream sleep caused disrupted concentration, anxiety, and irritability. Dement concluded that effective rest requires dreaming.

Discussion Questions
1. Explain how intrasubject and intersubject replication were used in this study.
2. Diagram this single subject ABAB reversal design.

SUGGESTED READINGS

Hall, C.S., Domhoff, W., Blick, K. A., & Weesner, K. E. (1982) The dreams of college men and women in 1950 and 1980: A comparison of dream contents and sex differences. *Sleep, 5,* 188-194.

ANSWERS

Fill-in: Self Test
1. Inferential
2. Single subject
3. Case study
4. Context
5. Retrospective
6. Control
7. Time series
8. Baseline
9. Operational definitions
10. Reversal
11. Independent
12. Multielement
13. Reversals
14. Stable
15. Counterbalancing

True/False: Self Test
1. False
2. True
3. False
4. True
5. False
6. True
7. False
8. True
9. False
10. True

Multiple Choice: Self Test

1. A
2. C
3. B
4. D
5. C
6. B
7. C
8. D
9. C
10. B
11. C
12. D
13. B
14. A
15. D
16. C

CHAPTER 13

Questionnaires, Survey Research and Sampling

CHAPTER OBJECTIVES: CONCEPT CHECKS

The chapter objectives provide you with a concept checklist. These are things you should know after reading Chapter 13. The accompanying text page numbers are reference aids for your review.

1. What are Campbell and Katona's nine steps for designing a survey? (296-297)

2. What can be gained from pretesting a survey? (301=302)

3. Explain the two main approaches to self-report data. (302-303)

4. What are the five main methods of administering a survey? Describe their advantages and disadvantages. (303-309)

5 Define the two main types of sampling. Give several specific examples of each. (311-313)

6. What two questions need to be asked to determine sample size? (314)

STUDY GUIDE AND REVIEW

Key Terms

Define each of these terms in your own words. Check your understanding of Chapter 13 by referring to the featured text page.

1. Open-ended question (297-298)

2. Fixed alternative (298)

3. Funneling (299)

4. Balanced response set (299)

5. Likert-type scale (299)

6. Item analysis (299-300)

7. Semantic differential (300)

8. Semantic space of experience (300)

9. Establishing context (301)

10. Leading questions (301)

11. Pretest (of a survey) (301-302)

12. Face-to-face interview (303-306)

13. Telephone interviews (306-307)

14. Mail questionnaires (307)

15. Computer survey

16. Internet survey

17. Sampling (309-314)

18. Census (310)

19. Population (310,294)

20. Sample (311)

21. Probability sampling (311-313)

22. Nonprobability sampling (313-314)

23. Simple random sampling (311)

24. Systematic random sampling (312)

25. Stratified random sampling (312)

26. Cluster sampling (312)

27. Multistage sampling (313)

28. Convenience sampling (313)

29. Quota sampling (313)

30. Snowball sampling (313-314)

31. Sample size (314)

32. Confidence interval (314)

33. Sampling error (314)

34. Reliability (315)

35. Validity (315)

Fill-in: Self Test

Fill in the missing word or phrase. Focus your attention on important Chapter 13 details.

1. Before the actual data are collected, it is important to specify the plan of analysis that will answer the research _____. (294)

2. Questions with no fixed answers that allow the respondent to answer in any manner are called _____ questions. (297-298)

3. Fixed alternative questions are also known as _____ questions. (298)

4. It is possible to combine open-ended and closed-ended questions in a single item by adding a(n) _____ category, which requests that the respondents add their own specific responses. (298)

5. When a researcher begins a line of questioning with a broad open-ended question and then follows with more specific items, this process is referred to as _____. (299)

6. Questions that ask for specific information like income should not have response categories that _____. (299)

7. A(n) _____ determines which items contribute to the index consistently across participants. (299)

8. The _____ was originally developed for measuring the semantic space of experience, by using adjectives that may be related experientially to a concept. (300)

9. One of the most important guidelines for survey research is to _____ the survey to check for ambiguity and misunderstanding of items. (301-302)

10. When administering a survey, typically one is faced with the trade-off between _____ and cost. (309)

11. A survey where the sample includes the entire population is referred to as a(n) _____. (310)

12. A(n) _____ is made from a sample to the population. (310)

13. A low variation or _____ population on the characteristic we wish to study will require fewer participants in the sample to generalize adequately. (314)

True/ False: Self Test

Test your understanding of Chapter 13 by marking the best answer to these true or false items.

1. _____ The manner of survey administration will often influence the format of the questions being asked because they are highly interrelated. (297)

2. _____ Once the actual questions are developed, it is important to pretest them to ensure clarity. (301-302)

3. _____ Open-ended questions offer an important way to begin a survey. (297-298)

4. _____ One of the advantages of the open-ended question is that the researcher's point of view is not imposing and does not threaten the probability of valid responses. (297-298)

5. _____ It is a problem to use open-ended questions followed by fixed alternatives. (297-299)

6. _____ One of the first rules of developing a questionnaire is to ask only what you need to know. (301)

7. _____ It is not common to pretest a survey more than once. (301)

8. _____ With regard to the disconnected approach to self-report data, it has been suggested that verbal data are important in their own right and do not have to be related to an observed behavior. (305)

9. _____ Psychological relationships are complex, yet are expected to show identical patterns in every situation. (305)

10. _____ Typically, the return rate of mail surveys is more than 50 percent. (307)

11. _____ The basic idea behind sampling is that we would like to learn about the characteristics of a large group of individuals by studying a smaller group. (310)

12. _____ According to the text, we want our sample to be as small as possible to be efficient in its use of time and money. (310)

13. _____ In general, the larger and more variable the population to which we want to generalize, the smaller the sample size. (311)

Multiple Choice: Self test

Test your Chapter 13 comprehension by circling the best answer to these multiple choice questions.

1. With respect to the sample, it is important to determine _____ before research begins. (310)

   a. which population will be addressed and to whom the study will be generalized
   b. how large the sample must be to address the research question
   c. how the sample will be chosen
   d. All of the above

2. According to Campbell and Katona (1953), what is the final stage of conducting a survey? (297)

   a. Tabulation
   b. Analysis and reporting
   c. Fieldwork
   d. Content analysis

3. "How do you think volunteerism has influenced your professional success?" is an example of what kind of question? (297-298)

   a. an open ended question
   b. a closed ended question
   c. a fixed alternative question
   d. a Likert-type question
   e. a semantic differential

4. One of the disadvantages of the open-ended question is that _____. (298)

    a. it is inflexible
    b. the person being interviewed may give you information that you have not requested
    c. the respondent is limited in his or her answers
    d. it poses a problem when you try to analyze the data and establish behavioral patterns

5. What is a disadvantage of fixed-alternative questions? (298)

    a. They are complex and difficult to score.
    b. The respondents can not give a reason for their responses.
    c. They are always limited to "Yes" or "No" answers.
    d. They can't be combined with open-ended questions.

6. A question that limits the number of responses that an individual can make is known as a(n) _____ question. (298)

    a. open-ended
    b. closed ended
    c. fixed-combination
    d. none of the above

7. A Likert-type scale is an example of _____. (299-300)

    a. a nonverbal alternative response format
    b. a fixed-alternative format
    c. a bipolar adjective format
    d. a weighted open-response scale

8. The following response format is an example of a(n) _____? (300)

How do you feel about research methods? Good .... Bad

    a. Likert item
    b. Likert-type item
    c. semantic differential item
    d. Thurstone item

9. Which of the following was suggested by Nisbett and Wilson (1977) regarding what people know about their own behavior? (305)

   a. Participants may be unaware of stimuli that may influence a response.
   b. Participants may be unaware of their own behavioral response.
   c. Participants may be unaware that a particular stimulus has actually influenced a particular response.
   d. All of the above

10. In comparison to other forms of survey administration, _____ have a higher completion rate and more complete information. (303)

   a. mail surveys
   b. telephone surveys
   c. face-to face interviews
   d. All of the above

11. What is a disadvantage of the face-to-face interview? (303, 306)

   a. It is very expensive in time and personnel.
   b. The interviewer may bias the results.
   c. The respondents may give different answers in face-to-face interviews than with an anonymous questionnaire.
   d. All of the above

12. When a lengthy session is needed to administer a survey that will require more than 15 minutes, which of the following would be inappropriate? (306)

   a. face-to-face interview
   b. telephone interview
   c. mail survey
   d. All of the above

13. A return rate of more than _____ should be considered acceptable in a mail survey. (307)

   a. 10%
   b. 25%
   c. 50%
   d. 95%

14. What action is called for when the return rate is low in the mail survey? (308)

    a. Reconsider the type of sample that is required.
    b. Reconsider the purpose of the survey.
    c. Reconsider the manner in which the survey is to be utilized.
    d. All of the above

15. To ensure that mail questionnaires are completed and returned, the text suggests including a _____. (308)

    a. hand written note
    b. cover letter
    c. postage paid return envelope
    d. Both b and c

16. What is one way of increasing the response rate in a mail survey? (308)

    a. Send a follow-up letter as a reminder to the respondent
    b. Send another copy of the questionnaire
    c. Send the survey to more people
    d. Both a and b

17. What are the aims of a census? (310)

    a. To obtain descriptive information concerning a particular group of individuals
    b. To generalize beyond the specific group from which they were obtained
    c. To use multistage sampling to obtain a sample that is characteristic of the population
    d. All of the above

18. According to the text, what are the two general types of sampling? (311-314)

    a. Probability and nonprobability sampling
    b. Systematic and nonsystematic sampling
    c. Convenience and nonconvenience sampling
    d. Descriptive and inferential sampling

19. This type of nonprobability sampling, which is referred to as _____, is most often used when no list or record of the population exists. (313-314)

    a. stratified random sampling
    b. snowball sampling
    c. cluster sampling
    d. systematic sampling

20. To examine the utilization of mental health care in rural and urban areas in Fresno, California you randomly select groups of participants who live in selected city blocks. This is an example of _____ sampling. (313)

    a. simple random
    b. stratified
    c. proportional
    d. snowball
    e. cluster

21. Which of the following are considered probability samples? (312-313)

    a. simple random sampling
    b. systematic sampling
    c. stratified random sampling
    d. cluster sampling
    e. All of the above

22. If you were interested in a study on homeless women with children, what kind of sampling would be most appropriate? (313-314)

    a. simple random sampling
    b. systematic sampling
    c. stratified random sampling
    d. quota sampling
    e. snowball sampling

Essays

Apply your knowledge of Chapter 13 as you analyze the following questions in detail. Specifically refer to information in the chapter to support your answers.

1. What are the steps outlined by Campbell and Katona (1953) for designing a survey research project?

2. Compare and contrast the characteristics of open-ended, and fixed alternative questions. Identify the advantages and limitations of each.

3. Discuss the importance of pretesting a survey. What should be addressed during this process?

4. Describe in detail the advantages and disadvantages of the following methods for survey administration: face-to-face interviews, telephone interviews, and mail questionnaires.

5. Discuss the defining features, and the strengths and weaknesses of each of the following:

   a. Probability sampling

      Simple random sampling

      Systematic sampling

      Stratified random sampling

      Cluster sampling

      Multistage sampling

   b. Nonprobability sampling

      Convenience sampling

      Quota sampling

      Snowball sampling

6. Describe the two main considerations that need to be addressed when selecting a sample size. In addition, discuss how the issue of accuracy in the estimate of population values relates to the concepts of confidence intervals, and sampling error.

7. If Nisbett and Wilson's (1977) research is supported, how would researchers need to rethink survey research?

8. Check out one of the websites mentioned in this chapter to learn more about Ainsworth's longitudinal study on attachment. What are three characteristics of this seminal survey research?

9. What are the advantages of taking a computer versus paper survey?

10. Participate in a short psychological internet survey. Describe the positives and negative aspects of this experience.

11. Compare and contrast reliability and validity.

RESEARCH ACTIVITIES

The goals of the research activities are to: (1) relate Chapter 13 on an applied learning dimension, and (2) get you involved in research.

1. **Sampling Method. Minority Attitudes on Controversial Legislation:** You are a researcher interested in the views of minority groups in the state regarding controversial legislative issues such as capital punishment, abortion-rights, and access to health care. The survey you have designed is quite lengthy, and due to the nature of the survey, you have decided that face-to-face interviews will be necessary.

   At this point you are trying to decide whether to use cluster sampling or multistage sampling for your research project. Develop specific plans that would be used for each sampling procedure, discuss the benefits/limitations of each, and report your decision on which of the two procedures you will use. Provide an explanation of the rational underlying your choice.

2. How are **Gallup polls** conducted? Search the internet for information about this process. Find information on the internet about a current Gallup poll. Report the poll's findings.

3. **AIDS Attitudes. Design a Questionnaire.** Fill in the following information.

   a. Flowchart the steps required for this assignment in your workbook. Refer to Campbell and Katona's steps for designing a survey research project. (312-313)

   b. Research other published work in this area for ideas and guidelines. List your references in APA format.

   c. Create questions. Write your ideas in your workbook.

   d. Develop ten question items that aim to assess attitudes about AIDS. Also include demographic questions.

   Question format: Your questionnaire should include at least one question from each of the following question formats: open-ended, fixed-alternative, and combined open- and closed-ended.

   Response Format: Your questionnaire should also include at least one example of each of the following response formats: Likert-type scale and semantic differential. Also demonstrate funneling.

   e. Format your AIDS survey in your workbook. Later type up your survey before administering it.

f. Pretest your questionnaire with at least five participants. In your workbook detail the problems that were identified in the pretest and how they may be corrected.

4. **Debate Hite's Survey Research.** *The Hite Report: Women and Love* (1987) has been a widely debated survey. Hite has been strongly criticized for her research techniques. Hite designed a completely open-ended survey consisting of 127 questions. A sample of 4,500 females voluntarily responded out of 100,000 surveys that were sent to various organizations nationwide to protect anonymity. The questionnaire begins: "Hello! Who are you? What is your description of yourself?" It continues with questions like the following: "Have you ever felt you were 'owned' or suffocated, held down in a relationship so that you wanted out?" and "Did you ever cry yourself to sleep because of problems with someone you loved? Why? Contemplate suicide? When were you the loneliest?" The most publicized findings were about women and extramarital sex. Hite reported that "70% of women married more than five years are having sex outside the marriage -- although most believe in monogamy." Interestingly, 95% of the women who responded said they had been emotionally or psychologically harassed by men they love. Hite claims three countries have replicated her study and found largely the same results.

Hite presented a paper, "Devising a New Methodological Framework for Analysis and Presentation of Data in Mixed Quantitative/ Qualitative Research," in May, 1985 to the American Association for the Advancement of Science in Washington, D.C. Hite is unlike scientific researchers who strive for objective and value-free findings.

Assignment: Research Hite's work (see the Suggested Readings) and published reviews of her work. Respond to the following questions in your workbook. Be prepared to debate this issue in class.

a. What is your opinion of Hite's research methodology?

b. What is her background?

c. Does she utilize random sampling?

d. What is your opinion of the response rate?

e. Do you feel her sample is representative of the population?

f. What do you think about her survey format?

g. Would you agree to respond to this survey?

h. What do you think is the motivation of the respondents?

i. Are her generalizations internally valid? Why or why not?

5. **Conduct a Survey. Death with Dignity.**

   A. Sample ten participants (N=10)

   B. Administer the following by either:

   (i) Face-to-face interview
   (ii) Telephone interview
   (iii) Mail survey. Include a cover letter and a self-addressed envelope.
   iv) Computer survey

   C. Record and tabulate the data. Reverse score all odd-numbered questions. For example: If a person marked "4" in response to question #1, you would reverse score by flipping the scale; thus the participant would now be given a value of "2" which will be used in the calculation of the overall score. A high overall score indicates a high positive attitude toward this issue.

   D. Research and find three references related to this topic.

   E. Report your findings in your workbook.

CONSENT

I am a student in a college-level research course. As part of my course work I am requesting your honest responses to the following statements. There are no right or wrong answers. I am most interested in learning about your attitudes on death-related issues. Your participation is voluntary and you may stop at any time. All responses are anonymous and will be used for educational purposes only. Thank you for participating.

DEATH WITH DIGNITY SCALE

1. All life holds value. People should not have the right to decide when they die.

1	2	3	4	5
Strongly Agree	Agree	Neutral	Disagree	Strongly Disagree

2. If someone tells a family member that he or she never wants to be kept alive on life support in the event of an accident, that decision should be respected regardless of the wishes of the family.

1	2	3	4	5
Strongly Agree	Agree	Neutral	Disagree	Strongly Disagree

3. Patients who request medical assistance to accelerate death are generally psychologically ill.

1	2	3	4	5
Strongly Agree	Agree	Neutral	Disagree	Strongly Disagree

4. Patients who suffer severe chronic pain due to a terminal condition should be able to request physician-assisted euthanasia legally.

1	2	3	4	5
Strongly Agree	Agree	Neutral	Disagree	Strongly Disagree

5. A physician is morally obligated to keep a patient alive at all costs.

1	2	3	4	5
Strongly Agree	Agree	Neutral	Disagree	Strongly Disagree

6. Legislation that guarantees the freedom to make individual choices in death is long overdue.

1	2	3	4	5
Strongly Agree	Agree	Neutral	Disagree	Strongly Disagree

7. **Family members should not be allowed to make life-and-death decisions on behalf of an individual who no longer has the ability to express their wishes.**

1	2	3	4	5
Strongly Agree	Agree	Neutral	Disagree	Strongly Disagree

8. **When a patient is in an irreversible vegetative state, he or she should be taken off life support and allowed to die without legal interference.**

1	2	3	4	5
Strongly Agree	Agree	Neutral	Disagree	Strongly Disagree

9. **Physicians who assist suicide at the request of a terminally ill patient should be criminally prosecuted for murder.**

1	2	3	4	5
Strongly Agree	Agree	Neutral	Disagree	Strongly Disagree

10. **Parents of terminally ill children should have the legal right to request medical action to induce a painless death for that child.**

1	2	3	4	5
Strongly Agree	Agree	Neutral	Disagree	Strongly Disagree

11. **What is your gender?**
    1=Male
    2=Female

12. **What is your year of birth?**

RESEARCH SUMMARY AND DISCUSSION QUESTIONS

Questionnaires, Survey Research, and Sampling

Back Off, Buddy. (October 12, 1987), *Time*, 68-73.

A well discussed survey in the 1980's on women's feelings toward sex, love, and relationships was conducted by Hite. She sent 100,000 surveys to women across the country. Four thousand five hundred women returned the survey (i.e., 4.5% response rate). Among Hite's findings were that 95% of women reported their male partners emotionally or psychologically harassed them; 98% said they desired more verbal closeness from their male partners; 70% of married women reported they were having an extramarital affair; and 87% of married women reported their deepest emotional relationship was with a woman friend.

Hite was highly criticized for her sampling procedures and radical feminist bias; however, supporters of Hite claimed that she had tapped a raw nerve among American women who were pervasively dissatisfied with love relationships.

Discussion Questions
1.   What is your impression of this survey? Comment on the question items and the tone of the survey.
2.   Discuss Hite's sampling method.

SUGGESTED READINGS

Dillman, D.A. (1978). *Mail and telephone surveys: The total design method*. New York: John Wiley and Sons.

Also check out Dillman's recent book on computer surveys called the tailored design method.

Hite, S. (1987). *Women and love*. New York: Alfred Knopf, Inc.

Hite, S. (1983). *The Hite report on male sexuality*. New York: Ballantine Books.

Hite, S. (1976). *The Hite report: A nationwide study on female sexuality*. New York: Macmillan.

ANSWERS

Fill-in: Self Test

1. Hypothesis
2. Open-ended
3. Closed-ended
4. "Other"
5. Funneling
6. Overlap
7. Item analysis
8. Semantic differential
9. Pretest
10. Response rate
11. Census
12. Inference
13. Homogeneous

True/False: Self Test

1. True
2. True
3. True
4. False
5. False
6. True
7. False
8. True
9. False
10. False
11. True
12. True
13. False

Multiple Choice: Self Test

1. D
2. B
3. A
4. D
5. B
6. B
7. B
8. C
9. D
10. C
11. D
12. B
13. C
14. D
15. D
16. D
17. A
18. A
19. B
20. E
21. E
22. E

CHAPTER 14

Ethics

CHAPTER OBJECTIVES: CONCEPT CHECKS

The chapter objectives provide you with a concept checklist. These are things you should know after reading Chapter 14. The accompanying text page numbers are reference aids for your review.

1. Discuss the balance between the rights of the scientist and the rights of the participant. (322-325)

2. What key issues must be addressed in the informed consent? (324)

3. What is the scientist's responsibility with respect to the participant's right to privacy? Address the issues of confidentiality and anonymity. (325)

4. What issues are outlined in the American Psychological Association's ethical guidelines? (326-328)

5. What is the purpose of the Institutional Review Board? What questions are likely to be asked by the board? (329-330)

6. Are there any possible drawbacks to be considered when using an informed consent? Discuss this issue in terms of the psychological evidence. (331-332)

7. How would you describe a deception study? What are the guidelines according to the American Psychological Association? (332)

8. Describe Milgram's study on obedience. Why was it controversial? (332-334)

9. Explain in detail the process of debriefing. (337-338)

10. Why is it useful for the scientist to consider the participant as a colleague? (338)

11. How can animals be protected against inhumane treatment in research? (339=344)

STUDY GUIDE AND REVIEW

<u>Key Terms</u>

Define each of these terms in your own words. Check your understanding of Chapter 14 by referring to the featured text page.

1. Ethics (320)

2. Kant's Imperative (320)

3. Nuremberg trials (323)

4. Informed consent (324)

5. Voluntary participation (323-324)

6. Right to privacy (325)

7. Private personality (325)

8. Confidentiality (325)

9. Anonymity (325)

10. Deception study (332)

11. Debriefing (337)

12. Participant as colleague (338)

13. Ethical principles in the use of animals (339-340)

Fill-in: Self Test

Fill in the missing word or phrase. Focus your attention on important Chapter 14 details.

1. Ethics may be explained as one aspect of the participant-scientist relationship as seen from the viewpoint of the _____. (320)

2. Ethics shift the focus of the experiment from observation and theory to the world of human _____. (320)

3. According to the text, how we view those involved in research may _____ the human qualities of those involved in the scientific enterprise. (322)

4. As a result of the _____, a code of ethics for human medical experimentation was adopted. (323)

5. A conversation between the participant and the scientist should not be made public without the participant's consent. This ethical principle respects the participant's right to _____. (324)

6. The right to have private thoughts is sometimes referred to as the right to have a(n) _____. (325)

7. Loftus and Fries (1979) argued that _____ may be hazardous to participants. They noted evidence that humans change their moods, attitudes, and feelings when presented with information detailing experimental procedures and potential risks. (331)

8. A study in which the participant is deceived about the purpose of the experiment or the experimental procedures is referred to as a(n) _____ study. (332)

9. The process of explaining the true purpose of the experiment after the participant has participated is referred to as _____. (337)

10. An alternative to conducting a deception study would be to inform the participants about the experiment and to ask them to act out or _____ the situation. (330)

11. Dawkins addresses the use of animals in research and the need for an objective definition of when an animal is suffering. She suggests that attention should be given to the _____ of the animals. (341)

True/False: Self Test

Test your understanding of Chapter 14 by marking the best answer to these true or false items.

1. _____ Participants participating in psychological research should not be harmed or affected in a way that would result in a lower level of any aspect of human functioning. (321)

2. _____ Ethical considerations in psychological research ignore the scientists' right to know and to seek answers to questions. (322-323)

3. _____ The voluntary participation principle includes a statement regarding the participant's right to withdraw from the experiment at any time without penalty. (323-324)

4. _____ A good working procedure in experimentation is to tell prospective participants about the experiment as fully as possible without jeopardizing the value of the study. (324-325)

5. _____ In our society, participants are considered to have the same rights during an experiment that they have outside the experiment. (325)

6. _____ The main task of the Institutional Review Board is to determine if the research has sound methodology and is justified. (329-330)

7. _____ Evidence supports the contention that knowledge of possible symptoms can not cause the onset of symptoms nor can knowledge of placebo effects. (331)

8. _____ In the Milgram study, voltage level was used as a measure of the participant's willingness to obey authority even in the face of pressure from the learner not to inflict pain. (332-334)

9. _____ According to Milgram's follow-up report, 84% of participants expressed negative feelings about their participation in the obedience to authority study. (334)

10. _____ According to federal guidelines for ethical care of animals in research, the investigator should consider that procedures that cause pain or distress in humans may cause pain or distress in other animals. (339-344)

11. _____ Treating a participant as a colleague recognizes the importance of the participant's help in acquiring valuable information about psychological processes. (338)

12. _____ The use of nonhuman animals in research requires similar considerations as with human participants. The federal government and the APA have guidelines for the care and use of animals in research. (339-344)

Multiple Choice: Self Test

Test your Chapter 14 comprehension by circling the best answer to these multiple choice questions.

1. Which of the following describes the current ethical status in experimentation? (320-322)

    a. Actual ethical problems are minimal in most psychological experimentation.
    b. Ethical decisions are somewhat regulated in our society by both the government and the American Psychological Association.
    c. There are no hard and fast ethical rules for every situation.
    d. All of the above

2. Is it ethical to require students to participate in psychological research? (323-324)

    a. It is ethical as long as they sign consent forms.
    b. It is ethical if you give them extra credit.
    c. It is unethical to require or otherwise coerce a participant to participate.
    d. Both a and b

3. What major ethical ingredient(s) does the witness look for in the dialogue between the participant and scientist? (323-324)

    a. Voluntary participation
    b. Informed consent
    c. Compensation
    d. Both a and b

4. What principle requires that the personal identity of a given participant be kept separate from his or her data? (325)

    a. Principle of confidentiality
    b. Principle of anonymity
    c. Principle of voluntary participation
    d. Both a and b

5. Which of the following procedures addresses participant anonymity? (325)

    a. The participant's name is not requested.
    b. Coding procedures are utilized for identification.
    c. The list of participant's names is destroyed once the data analysis has been completed.
    d. All of the above

6. This group directly provides guidelines in psychological experimentation addressing the right of participants not to be harmed. (326-330)

    a. The American Psychological Association
    b. The Institutional Review Board
    c. The International Human Rights Committee
    d. Both a and b

7. Who has the primary responsibility for ensuring the ethical treatment of subjects in the experimental setting? (329)

    a. The American Psychological Association
    b. The Institutional Review Board
    c. The researcher
    d. All of the above

8. How do the APA guidelines view deception in research? (327-329)

    a. Research using deception is "at risk" and not ethical.
    b. Research using deception is acceptable only when it is justified and alternative procedures are not feasible.
    c. Research using deception is unconditionally acceptable and often used for valid psychological research.
    d. No psychological research using deception has been approved since the public outcry in response to the Milgram study.

9. What major question(s) concern(s) the Institutional Review Board? (329-332)

    a. Are the risks to the subject outweighed by the potential benefits to society?
    b. Are the risks to the subject unreasonable?
    c. Are there potential long-term effects?
    d. All of the above

10. Which of the following procedures did Milgram use in his Obedience to Authority study? (332-334)

    a. Participants were fully debriefed.
    b. Participants had a friendly reconciliation with the "learners" and had an opportunity to discuss the experiment.
    c. Participants were assured that their behavior was normal and the tension they felt was felt by other participants.
    d. All of the above

11. What is the purpose of debriefing? (337-338)

    a. To provide an opportunity for participants to tell the experimenter how they felt about being part of the experiment
    b. To provide an opportunity for the experimenter to explain the study to the participants in greater detail
    c. In the case of deception research, to allow the researcher to discuss the reason why deception was necessary
    d. All of the above

12. Which of the following is true regarding the attitudes of participants in the Milgram study? (334)

    a. 80% believed Milgram was unethical.
    b. 80% believed this type of research should be carried out.
    c. 74% said they had learned something of personal importance from their participation in the experiment.
    d. Both b and c

13. What is an alternative to the use of animals in high-risk experimentation? (339-344)

    a. Computer simulation
    b. Mathematical models
    c. In vitro methods
    d. All of the above

14. What were the conclusions of Baumrind (1964) in reference to the Milgram study? (333)

    a. Baumrind suggests that the participants were treated with respect.
    b. Baumrind felt the participants were manipulated and made to experience emotional disturbances.
    c. Baumrind suggests that participants should have signed an informed consent.
    d. All of the above

15. In what way are the rights of the participant considered in experimentation? (323-324)

    a. Through the principle of voluntary participation
    b. Through the principle of informed consent
    c. Though the principle of compensation
    d. Both a and b

16. What information is required in an informed consent? (324-325)

    a. The participant must be informed of what will be expected of him or her
    b. The participant must be informed of the potential risks that may result from participation
    c. The participant must be informed of his or her constitutional rights
    d. Both a and b

17. The process after experimentation whereby participants are told about the importance of their participation and the reasons for any deception is referred to as _____. (337)

    a. informed consent
    b. debriefing
    c. manipulation check
    d. desensitization

18. To conduct ethical research using human participants, what must be ensured? (323-325)

    a. Participation must be voluntary.
    b. Participants must be informed of their rights.
    c. Participants must be informed about any potential risks.
    d. All of the above

19. What are the ethical guidelines related to deception in research? (332-334)

    a. Deception is not ethical and not permitted.
    b. Deception can only be used in studies that are minimal risk.
    c. Deception may be used only if alternative procedures are not feasible.
    d. Deception can be used without restriction but participants must be debriefed.
    e. Deception that influences one's financial or legal status may not be used, otherwise deception is permissible.

20. What studies require institutional review? (329-332)

    a. All university studies require institutional review for ethical protocol.
    b. Only deception studies must be reviewed for ethical protocol.
    c. Only medical and psychological studies require institutional review.
    d. None of the above

Essays

Apply your knowledge of Chapter 14 as you analyze the following questions in detail. Specifically refer to information in the chapter to support your answers.

1. Discuss your views on the ethics of using prisoners, children, and mental patients as participants in psychological experimentation.

2. Discuss the difference between informed consent and educated consent. Give examples to illustrate when an informed consent may not necessarily be an educated consent.

3. Discuss the ideas/evidence presented by Loftus and Fries. Your response should include information regarding suggestibility and placebo effects. (350-351)

4. Do you believe that the purpose of informed consent is to protect participants from harm, to protect investigators and institutions from lawsuits due to the consequences of deception, or both? Defend your answer.

5. Discuss the issue of debriefing using APA principles 6.15 and 6.18 as well as other information from the text. In addition, describe your beliefs on whether these ethical principles are adequate in the case of studies using deception.

6. What major questions will the Institutional Review Board address in the review of research proposals?

7. What do you think about Milgram's Obedience to Authority study? Explain your position and refer to the APA ethical guidelines.

8. How was science advanced by the Milgram experiment? How would you change the ethical procedures of this study? Do you think the ethically revised study would find such dramatic results? Would this study be approved by the institutional review board at your college?

9. How do you feel about the use of animals as subjects in research? What changes to the current guidelines would you recommend for future animal experimentation?

10. Is plagiarism part of the APA ethical guidelines? Explain.

RESEARCH ACTIVITIES

The goals of the research activities are to: (1) relate Chapter 14 on an applied learning dimension, and (2) get you involved in research.

1. **Debate the Tea Room Trade Study.** Humphreys (1970) studied the homosexual encounters of men in public restrooms. In this study he participated as someone who keeps watch for the police or strangers entering the restroom while observing sexual acts. Though the men were unaware that they were being studied, the investigator asked questions of some of the men and recorded their license plate numbers. With this information he located their names and addresses. He later went to their home residence posing as a health service worker and requested information regarding their family, occupation, and social life.

    Assignment: In your workbook present your position on this study. A reference is provided in the Suggested Readings. Refer to the APA ethical guidelines to support your answer. Address the issues of deception, informed consent, and voluntary participation. Further discuss the potential risks to the subject. Did the risks outweigh the experimental benefits? Be prepared to debate this issue in class.

Issue	Risks	APA Ethical Principle
Deception		
Informed Consent		
Voluntary Participation		

    Discuss
    Analysis of the Risk/Benefit Ratio
    Suggestions for changing the study

2. **Develop an Informed Consent.** In your workbook write an informed consent on an original research topic or on a published research article of your choice.

INFORMED CONSENT CHECKLIST

1. Who is the investigator and what is his or her affiliation?

2. What is the purpose of the research and why is it important?

3. What are the experimental procedures? How long will they take? What will the participant be expected to do? Where will the experiment take place?

4. What are the potential risks and/or discomforts? How are these risks managed?

5. How will the findings of this study benefit the participant and the public?

6. State the terms of confidentiality and/or anonymity. How will they be managed?

7. Inform the participant of the right to withdraw at any time without penalty.

8. If appropriate, state how the participant will be compensated for participation.

9. Inform the participant of the investigator's willingness to answer any questions. Provide a contact for the participant to request follow-up information.

10. Provide a place for the signature of the participant and the date.

3. **Animal Subjects in Research.** Research groups like the People for the Ethical Treatment of Animals, the Animal Rights Coalition, and the Society Against Vivisection have strongly protested the use of animals in research.

   Assignment:
   (A) Using InfoTrac, locate information about the major concerns of these groups. In you workbook discuss why they have targeted psychological research as being especially abusive towards animals.

   (B) Using InfoTrac, find two published psychological articles about studies that utilized animal subjects. Record the references in your workbook. The *Journal of Experimental Psychology*, the *Journal of Comparative and Physiological Psychology*, and the *Journal of the Experimental Analysis of Behavior* may provide you with this information. Summarize the ethical treatment of animal subjects as described by the research investigator.

4. **Stanford Prison Study.** Research the "Stanford Prison Study" conducted by Zimbardo in the 1970's. Summarize the results of this study and cite information regarding Zimbardo's extensive debriefing procedures. Discuss your views on the ethics of conducting this study. Do you believe that the information gained from this research warranted the potential risks to the participants? Could this type of information be obtained through different means? If so, describe such alternative possibilities.

   In addition, respond to Zimbardo's statement made following the termination of the study: "In less than one week, the experience of imprisonment ended (temporarily) a lifetime of learning; human values were suspended, self-concepts were challenged, and the ugliest, most base, pathological side of human nature surfaced..."

5. **Research Misconduct**
   Use Infotrac to learn more about the prevalence of research misconduct and ethical violations in research. How widespread is it? What agency is ultimately responsible for ethical violations in research?

RESEARCH SUMMARY AND DISCUSSION QUESTIONS

Ethics

Milgram, S. (1963). Behavioral study of obedience. *Journal of Abnormal and Social Psychology, 67*, 371-378.

Milgram's study on obedience to authority rocked the scientific community. Milgram found that the majority of people would obey the orders of an authority even if it meant seriously hurting others. Ray noted in Chapter 14 that this study was highly criticized on ethical grounds. It was, however, a catalyst in the formation of policies to protect human participants involved in scientific research.

Discussion Questions
1.   Discuss how the rights of the research participants were violated in this study? How did Milgram manage participant's rights?
2.   Imagine yourself as a member of an Institutional Review Board. How would you evaluate this study based on the guidelines in Chapter 14.

SUGGESTED READINGS

Haney, C., Banks, C. & Zimbardo, P. (1973). Interpersonal dynamics in a simulated prison. *International Journal of Criminology and Penology, 1*, 69-87.

Holmes, D. S. (1976a). Debriefing after psychological experiments I: Effectiveness of postdeception dehoaxing. *American Psychologist, 31*, 858-867.

Holmes, D. S. (1976b). Debriefing after psychological experiments II: Effectiveness of postdeception desensitizing. *American Psychologist, 31*, 868-875.

Humphreys, L. (1970). *Tearoom trade*. Chicago: Aldine.

Jones, J. H. (1981). *Bad blood: The Tuskegee syphilis experiment*. New York: Free Press.

McArdle, J. (1984). Psychological experimentation on animals: Not necessary, not valid. *The Humane Society News, 29*, 20-22.

Milgram, S. (1974). *Obedience to authority*. New York: Harper & Row

This classic study stirred the scientific community.

ANSWERS

Fill-in: Self Test
1. Witness
2. Values
3. Depersonalize
4. Nuremberg
5. Privacy
6. Private personality
7. Informed consent
8. Deception
9. Debriefing
10. Role-play
11. Inner experience

True/False: Self Test
1. True
2. False
3. True
4. True
5. True
6. False
7. False
8. True
9. False
10. True
11. True
12. True

Multiple Choice: Self Test

1.   D
2.   C
3.   D
4.   B
5.   D
6.   D
7.   C
8.   B
9.   D
10. D
11. D
12. D
13. D
14. B
15. D
16. D
17. B
18. D
19. C
20. A

CHAPTER 15

Sharing the Results

CHAPTER OBJECTIVES: CONCEPT CHECKS

The chapter objectives provide you with a concept checklist. These are things you should know after reading Chapter 15. The accompanying text page numbers are reference aids for your review.

1. Discuss the idea that science is a shared activity. How was this emphasized by Aristotle? (349)

2. What two audiences must the scientist address in communicating research findings? How are the audiences benefited by this? (349)

3. What is the five-part format of the scientific article? (350)

4. What is the objective of the abstract? What essential information must be provided in this section? Describe the abstract with respect to its length and the amount of detail that is required. (351-353)

5. What is the purpose of the introduction? How is it organized? What five tasks does the introduction perform? (353-356)

6. What is the goal of the method section? Describe the three subsections. Is it appropriate to include the operational definition of your independent and dependent variables in this section? (356-360)

7. What is the chief purpose of the results section? Should you include an interpretation of the data analysis in this section? (360-362)

8. What are the three subsections of the discussion section? What information should be included in each part? (362-364)

9. How important is a good title? What should a good title include? (364)

10. How does the reference section benefit other scientists? Discuss the three purposes of the reference section. (364-366)

11. Explain the process of peer review when submitting an article for publication. What are the criteria for reviewer evaluation? (366)

12. According to Kazdin, what questions should guide the preparation of a good article? (369-370)

13. According to Mahler (1978), what is the most common reason an article is rejected for publication? According to your text, if an article is accepted, about how long will it take to get it into print? (370)

STUDY GUIDE AND REVIEW

Key Terms

Define each of these terms in your own words. Check your understanding of Chapter 15 by referring to the featured text page.

1. Scientific article (349-351)

2. Abstract (351-353)

3. Introduction (353-356)

4. Method (356-360)

5. Replication (356)

6. Participants (357)

7. Apparatus (357)

8. Procedure (358-359)

9. Results (360-3462)

10. Discussion (362-364)

11. Title (364)

12. References (364-366)

13. Peer review system (366)

14. Publication lag (368)

Fill-in: Self Test

Fill in the missing word or phrase. Focus your attention on important Chapter 15 details.

1. One important responsibility of the scientist is _____ , which explains new facts to other scientists and nonscientists. (349)

2. The actual experiment or observation that generates new ideas is described by Aristotle as _____ . (349)

3. The purpose of one section of the scientific article is to give a brief overall description of the experiment so that the reader can decide whether to read further or not. This section, which is at the beginning of a journal article, is called the _____ . (351)

4. In a(n) _____ study, the purpose of the research might be presented in the form of goals instead of hypotheses. (355)

5. The _____ section begins with a broad statement about the research topic and progresses to a specific statement of the research hypothesis. (353-354)

6. The goal of the method section is to provide enough detail for another researcher to conduct an exact _____ of your experiment. (356)

7. The chief purpose of the _____ section is to present the statistical outcome and then indicate whether the outcome was statistically significant. (360)

8. Frequently the results section contains _____ that aid the reader in descriptively visualizing the outcome. (360)

9. Any _____ presented in the introduction should have corresponding results presented in the results section. (360)

10. An interpretation of the findings is found in the _____ section of a scientific article. (362-364)

11. The _____ of your article should be created to specifically describe the nature of the experiment. It should also include the independent and dependent variables and their relationship. (364)

12. The process of review by other scientists is referred to as the _____ system. (366-368)

13. According to Mahler, most scientific articles are rejected for _____ reasons. (370)

14. The wait for an accepted scientific article to come into print is referred to as the
    _____. (368)

True/False: Self Test

Test your understanding of Chapter 15 by marking the best answer to these true or false items.

1. _____ A typical abstract provides a clear statement of the purposes of the study, the methodology, and the results. (351-352)

2. _____ The general format of the introduction is to begin with a specific statement of the hypothesis and to progressively discuss the topic from a specific to a general viewpoint. (353-356)

3. _____ Procedural details in the method section tell how the experiment was specifically conducted. However, this section does not generally provide enough information to identify design problems. (356-360)

4. _____ It is important to be selective in writing the method section and to not include information on every detail that the participants were told or were led to believe. (357-360)

5. _____ The important social characteristics of the experimenter and the manner in which she treated participants should be included in the method section of a journal article. (356-360)

6. _____ It is appropriate to include mean scores and standard deviations of scales used in assigning high and low conditions in the results section. (360)

7. _____ In a deception study, the investigator should include information on the safeguards, debriefing and follow-up procedures, such as in the methodology section of the scientific article. (358)

8. _____ The chief purpose of the results section is to explain and then interpret the findings of the experiment. (360)

9. _____ If your study is a replication or a continuation of some of the studies cited in your introduction, then probably the same journal that published the other study would not be interested in your work. (366)

10. _____ Journals may differ in the way they present the reference and results section. (366)

11. _____ According to the text, the publication lag may range from a month or two to over a year. (368)

Multiple Choice: Self Test

Test your Chapter 15 comprehension by circling the best answer to these multiple choice questions.

1. The idea that science is a shared activity is by no means new. More than 2000 years ago Aristotle emphasized that science had two parts: _____ and _____. (349)

   a. Exploration and summary
   b. Inquiry and argument
   c. Theoretical and applied
   d. Statistical significance and scientific significance

2. According to the text, to whom should the scientist direct her communication? (349)

   a. Scientists and nonscientists
   b. Theoretical and applied investigators
   c. Academic professionals and students of science
   d. All of the above

3. In what way is communication shared with other scientists? (349)

   a. Informal conversations
   b. Oral presentations at scientific meetings
   c. Published journal articles
   d. All of the above

4. Which of the following is required in preparing your research article? (349-351)

   a. A description of what is already known about the phenomenon being studied
   b. A clear statement of the purpose of the experiment
   c. Results of the experiment interpreted in relation to themselves and in relation to what we know about the phenomenon
   d. All of the above

5. The first section of a scientific journal is a summary of the entire article in about 100 to 150 words. This is referred to as the _____. (351)

   a. introduction
   b. synopsis
   c. abstract
   d. brief

6. What should be included in the abstract? (351-352)

   a. key words
   b. a summary of the article
   c. 100 to 150 words
   d. a clear statement of purpose
   e. All of the above

7. The introduction should begin with two sentences that explain the _____. (353)

   a. problem statement
   b. hypotheses
   c. procedure
   d. theories
   e. All of the above

8. This section of the scientific journal begins a description of the research in broad terms and then concludes by clearly identifying the research hypothesis. This section is identified as the _____. (353)

   a. abstract
   b. introduction
   c. methodology
   d. discussion

9. What must be included in the introduction? (353-356)

   a. relevant background
   b. purpose of the research
   c. why further research is necessary
   d. predictions and hypotheses
   e. All of the above

10. Which of the following is not a task specific to the introduction section? (353-356)

   a. Describes the relevant background
   b. Discusses the meaning of the study and its limitation
   c. Makes predictions and states the hypothesis
   d. Justifies the study

11. What are the three parts of the method section? (356-360)

    a. Sampling, Tests, Instructions
    b. Independent Variable, Dependent Variable, Operational Definitions
    c. Participants, Apparatus, Procedures
    d. Selection, Equipment, Experimentation

12. What is important to include in the participants subsection? (356-357)

    a. A description of the participants
    b. Number of participants
    c. Selection of participants
    d. All of the above

13. What section of an APA scientific article should include the operational definitions of the independent and dependent variables? (360)

    a. Abstract
    b. Introduction
    c. Method
    d. Results

14. What section would include information about whether the study was performed blind or if the experimenter who tested the participants knew to which group a given participant belonged? (360=362)

    a. Introduction
    b. Method
    c. Results
    d. Discussion

15. Which of the following is necessary to include in the discussion section? (362-364)

    a. Exploration of limitations and potential confounds that might affect the interpretation of the study
    b. How the study relates to other scientific investigations
    c. How the study contradicts or is inconsistent with other studies
    d. All of the above

16. What is the purpose of the reference section? (364-366)

   a. To acknowledge a documented scientific fact or working hypothesis
   b. To direct the reader to a more detailed discussion of a theoretical concept or a specific experimental/statistical procedure
   c. To give credit to other scientists for developing an idea, technique, or line of research
   d. All of the above

17. Which of the following is an important part of the evaluation of an article by a reviewer? (368)

   a. Clarity of presentation
   b. Logic of the experiment
   c. Appropriateness of data analysis
   d. All of the above

Essays

Apply your knowledge of Chapter 15 as you analyze the following questions in detail. Specifically refer to information in the chapter to support your answers.

1. Explain how both scientists and nonscientists can benefit from research findings. Illustrate with a recent example.

2. Describe the specific types of issues addressed in the five main parts of a scientific article as well as the reference section. Clearly state the purpose of each section. Include information related to Kazdin's guidelines for article publication in your response.

3. Most published scientific articles report finding statistical significance. Is there any benefit to communicating research that does not find statistical significance?

4. Why is it important to have strict guidelines for writing scientific research reports?

5. What information is important to include in a journal reference? Give an example.

6. Discuss the process required for publishing a journal article. Your response should include a discussion of the peer review system and publication lag.

RESEARCH ACTIVITIES

The goals of the research activities are to: (1) relate Chapter 15 on an applied learning dimension, and (2) get you involved in research.

1. **Correct APA Format.**

   Assignment: Correct the following abstract and references, using correct APA format.

   Abstract:

   The five factor model of personality (Goldberg; 1990, Digman; 1990) is a robust model that globally circumscribes the sphere of personality. Goldberg, 1990, 1981, proposes that this model represents 5 important dimensions that individuals use to evaluate others in the interpersonal environment. Indeed, the five factors arose out of analyses of adjectives used to describe personality. The factors are: 1. extroversion, 2. neuroticism, 3. conscientiousness, 4. openness to experience, and 5. agreeableness.

   250 introductory psychology students filled out a questionnaire to assess the 5 factors. Examination of the demographic data available indicated that twenty-eight percent of the participants were Oriental or Spanish-speaking. 79% of the participants were girls. A multivariate analysis of variance was used to examine cultural differences on all self- and peer-report scales. A significant multivariate effect was found for culture, F, 18, 162, = 2.144 at a .01 alpha level.

   Bibliography

   1. Goldberg, L.R. (1981). "Language and Individual differences: the search for universals in Personality lexicons." In L. Wheeler (Editor), Review of Personality and Social Psychology (Vol. 2, pp 141-165). Beverly Hill, CA; Sage.

   2. Digman, J. M. 1990. Personality Structure: Emergence of the Five-Factor Model. In M.R. Rosenzweig and L.W. Porter (eds.), Annual Review of Psychology (vol. 41, pp. 417-440). Palo Alto, CA: Annual Reviews.

   3. Goldberg, L. (1990) An alternative "description of personality": the big-five factor structure. Journal of personality and social psychology, 59, 1216-1229.

2. **Critique an APA Journal Article.** The purpose of this activity is to learn to dissect and analyze a scientific report. Further, oral presentations are an important means of communicating research findings at professional conventions. This activity will give you valuable experience and feedback.

Assignment: Organize a concise presentation analyzing a published research article of your choice. This assignment will also include a written summary and a copy of the original article to be turned in to your instructor. You may utilize visual aids. The length of the presentation should not exceed ten minutes. Be prepared to answer questions. Presentation dates will be randomly assigned.

You will graded on the following criteria:

1. Degree of difficulty.

2. Ability to identify the research hypothesis, variables, and type of study.

3. Ability to clearly describe the details of the research methodology.

4. Evidence of understanding statistical terms and techniques.

5. Clearly explaining important tables and figures.

6. Ability to identify limitations and weaknesses.

7. Evidence of creative thought in making recommendations.

8. Interesting, organized and thoughtful presentation.

9. Ability to answer questions from instructor and colleagues.

10. Written summary of the report.

3. **Research Proposal.**
   Assignment: Organize a research proposal following the guidelines of the Institutional Review Board (IRB). You may utilize either: (1) an original research idea that you have been developing during this course, or (2) a published research study. Outline the following in your workbook.

   CHECKLIST FOR RESEARCH PROPOSALS:

   A. **Application Forms**: (Your instructor will provide these as needed).

   B. **Abstract:** A brief summary that includes the research question, the proposed methodology, the recognized limitations, and the expected results.

   C. **Introduction**: Justify the study. List several references (APA format) in your workbook that you will use to support the research idea. State the research hypothesis.

   D. **Methodology**:

      1. **Participants**: Who will be the participants? How many do you need? How will you get them?

      2. **Tests**: Name the tests that you will be giving your participants in your workbook. Officially you will be required to include a copy of the actual tests and instructions to the IRB.

      3. **Procedure**: What are the experimental plans? Name the tests you will use. What will be required of the participants? Where will the experiment take place? How long will it take?

      4. **Risks and Benefits**: What are the potential risks to the participant? Are they beyond the risks of everyday living? What are the benefits to society? What are the benefits to the participant? Do the benefits outweigh the risks?

      5. **Risk Management**: What will you specifically do to respect the rights of the participant during experimentation? Informed consent? Anonymous responses? Coding procedures?

      6. **Compensation:** How will the participants be compensated? Extra credit? Research experience? Snacks? Money?

      7. **Informed Consent**: List the major issues you must address in the informed consent. Officially you must provide a copy of your informed consent to the IRB.

4.   **Peer Review. Romantic Interpersonal Relationships.** Go to the library and obtain a recent article on romantic interpersonal relationships.

Using Kazdin's guidelines for publishing journal articles, critique the article selected and describe how the author satisfies/fails to satisfy these guidelines. Finally, consider yourself a peer reviewer of this article. Evaluate the article according to the guidelines suggested in the chapter. Discuss limitations of the study as well as specific suggestions for improvement of the article. Provide a recommendation regarding whether the article should be published. Defend your answer.

5.   **Avoid Biased Wording**
How would you describe the following based on the current guidelines in the APA publication manual?

a.   older people
b.   gays
c.   subjects

RESEARCH SUMMARY AND DISCUSSION QUESTION

Sharing the Results

Ault, R. (1991). What goes where? An activity to teach the organization of journal articles. *Teaching of Psychology, 18,* 45-46.

In Chapter 15, Ray discussed the importance of sharing scholarly information with others in science. He also detailed the format that psychological scientists use to report empirical findings (i.e., APA format). The critical components of an APA research article are the title page, abstract, introduction section, methods, results, discussion section, and references.
Ault's article teaches APA style writing using a hands-on approach. As an activity Ault helps you organize information in the correct locations, and to learn about the writing conventions of APA style.

Discussion Questions
1.   Discuss the objectives of each section of an APA article.
2.   Make an outline of each section and detail the main objectives of each.

SUGGESTED READINGS

American Psychological Association. (1994) *Publication manual of the American Psychological Association.* Washington, D. C.: American Psychological Association.

Bond, L., & Magistrale, A. (1987). *A writer's guide to psychology.* New York: Heath & Co.

ANSWERS

Fill-in: Self Test
1. Communication
2. Inquiry
3. Abstract
4. Exploratory
5. Introduction
6. Replication
7. Results
8. Tables and figures
9. Hypothesis
10. Discussion
11. Title
12. Peer review
13. Methodological
14. Publication lag

True/False: Self Test
1. True
2. False
3. False
4. False
5. True
6. False
7. True
8. False
9. False
10. True
11. True

Multiple Choice: Self Test
1. B
2. A
3. D
4. D
5. C
6. E
7. A
8. B
9. C
10. B
11. B
12. C
13 D
14. C
15. B
16. D
17. D
18. D
19. C

CHAPTER 16

Beyond Method

CHAPTER OBJECTIVES: CONCEPT CHECKS

The chapter objectives provide you with a concept checklist. These are things you should know after reading Chapter 16. The accompanying text page numbers are reference aids for your review.

1. Explain the three dimensions of research approaches. (374-376)

2. Compare the advantages and disadvantages of the naturalistic and the experimental method. (375)

3. Explain the differing characteristics of laboratory and field research. (375)

4. Discuss the scientist as an observer and the scientist as a participant. (375)

5. What are three potential obstacles that may limit research? (377-381)

6. What did Lakatos suggest as a method to advance science? (377)

7. Distinguish between Lakatos' progressive and degenerative research programs. (377)

8. Describe Chamberlin's two fundamental approaches to learning. (382-383)

9. What is the objective of multiple working hypotheses? (383)

10. Explain the difference between statistical significance and scientific significance. (385)

11. Explain how scientific knowledge can be considered a superior knowledge. (386-388)

STUDY GUIDE AND REVIEW

<u>Key Terms</u>

Define each of these terms in your own words. Check your understanding of Chapter 16 by referring to the featured text page.

1. True experiment (374-375)

2. Active method (375-375)

3. Naturalistic observation (374-375)

4. Passive method (374)

5. Lab research (375)

6. Field research (375)

7. Research program (376)

8. Limitations due to tools (377-378)

9. Personal psychological limitations (380-381)

10. Progressive research program (377)

11. Degenerating research program (377)

12. Limitations due to tacit, metaphysical or unconscious views (378-380)

13. Thought experiment (382)

14. Multiple working hypotheses (383)

15. Universal values (383-385)

16. Relevance of findings (385)

17. Scientifically significant (385)

18. Statistically significant (385)

Fill-in: Self Test

Fill in the missing word or phrase. Focus your attention on important Chapter 16 details.

1. A true experiment studies the relationship between variables by directly manipulating an independent variable. This is defined by the text as a(n) _____ method. (374-375)

2. A passive method attempts to describe behavioral relationships as they occur spontaneously in their natural environment. This illustrates a(n) _____ observation. (374-375)

3. There is less control in field research than in laboratory research, but field research has more _____ validity. (375)

4. A series of directed research studies is referred to as a(n) _____. (376)·

5. According to Lakatos, research that leads in new directions and predicts new facts is characteristic of _____ research. (377)

6. According to Lakatos, a(n) _____ research program only reinterprets known facts in light of a given theory. (377)

7. This method considers a family of hypotheses, each leading to different conclusions or interpretations and is referred to as _____. (383)

8. Throughout the brief history of scientific psychology, we have focused our energy on the study of external behavior -- although originally psychology also explored personal _____. (386-387)

True/False: Self Test

Test your understanding of Chapter 16 by marking the best answer to these true or false items.

1. _____ The text suggests using both the experimental method and naturalistic observation simultaneously. (375)

2. _____ Scientists acknowledge the true experimental approach as the single most superior approach in studying all research questions. (374-375)

3. _____ Science is simply the application of an experimental method. (375)

4. _____ An obstacle that limits the finding of scientific answers is the personal psychological limitations of the scientist. (380-381)

5. _____ Although we are influenced in science by values, we in no way test the validity of these ethical and moral values. (383)

6. _____ It is possible to achieve statistically significant differences in science that are scientifically insignificant. (385)

7. _____ Science can be viewed only as value-free. (384)

8. _____ Methods are useful only in relation to a particular question being asked. (375)

9. _____ Technically, all research is progressive. (377)

10. _____ Psychology has become more inclusive of evolutionary perspectives and the role of genetics in explaining behavior. (386-388)

Multiple Choice: Self Test

Test your Chapter 16 comprehension by circling the best answer to these multiple choice questions.

1. A disadvantage of the naturalistic observation method is _____. (375)

   a. it is impossible to produce change in the participants being studied
   b. behavior must be studied as it occurs spontaneously
   c. it is unable to infer important relationships
   d. All of the above

2. According to the text, which research setting is the least influenced by demand characteristics? (375)

   a. The lab setting
   b. The field setting
   c. The group survey setting
   d. All of the above are highly susceptible to demand characteristics.

3. Which of the following represents an important research limitation in our search for answers? (377-378)

   a. The tools available to us
   b. The lack of communication within the scientific community
   c. The lack of applied models
   d. All of the above

4. What fundamental approach was suggested by Chamberlin in learning about the world? (382-383)

   a. Learning through imitation of the processes of previous thinkers
   b. Learning through independent creative study
   c. Learning by developing value-free methods that are relevant to the world we live in
   d. Both a and b

5. The need to distinguish between scientifically significant results and results that are statistically significant addresses the broad question of _____ in science. (385)

   a. limitations
   b. relevance
   c. transcendence
   d. All of the above

6. The inadequacy of theories is a view held by _____. (386)

   a. Karl Popper
   b. G. Spencer-Brown
   c. Thomas Kuhn
   d. All of the above

7. Who said "There are probably no questions we can think up that can't be answered, sooner or later"? (387)

   a. Karl Popper
   b. G. Spencer-Brown
   c. Lewis Thomas
   d. Thomas Kuhn

8. The text states "It is through the interplay of these three aspects that science comes alive." This refers to the interplay between _____. (386)

   a. scientist, participant, and witness
   b. value, relevance, and transcendence
   c. tools, shared views, and psychological limitations
   d. All of the above

9. Research is a multifaceted process. According to the text, which of the following represents an important dimension in research? (374-375)

    a. The dimension related to the research setting
    b. The dimension related to the type of methodology
    c. The dimension related to the role of the experimenter
    d. All of the above

10. How do the scientist's values influence her research? (383-385)

    a. Values influence how a scientist performs research.
    b. Values influence how a scientist interprets the scientific findings.
    c. Values influence what type of research the scientist chooses to pursue.
    d. All of the above

11. According to Lakatos, what is the main characteristic of progressive research? (377)

    a. It predicts novel facts.
    b. It reinterprets facts in light of new theories.
    c. It is strictly objective and value-free.
    d. All of the above

12. Which of the following does not represent one of the four fields of knowing in psychology? (386-388)

    a. How do I study my own experience?
    b. How do I study your experience?
    c. How do I study your behavior?
    d. All of these are listed in the text as fields of knowing.

13. Why does Ray consider science a superior form of knowledge? (386-388)

    a. Science is value-free.
    b. Science is without limitations.
    c. Science always progresses.
    d. Science is constantly questioning and revising.

Essays

Apply your knowledge of Chapter 16 as you analyze the following questions in detail. Specifically refer to information in the chapter to support your answers.

1. Explain Ray's three-dimensional approach to the research process.

2. What does Lakatos mean when he says "science is more than following trial and error hypotheses"?

3. Discuss the contrasting views of Lakatos and Kuhn regarding changes in science. Which view do you support? Provide historical examples and future predictions to illustrate your position.

4. Discuss why Ray believes scientific knowledge represents a superior knowledge.

5. If science strives to be objective, why is it not viewed as value-free?

6. Describe in detail and give examples of the three main limitations confronted by researchers.

7. Discuss and give examples of Chamberlin's two fundamental approaches to learning about the world. Explain the method he referred to as multiple working hypotheses and describe how it is similar to Platt's method of strong inference presented in Chapter 3.

RESEARCH ACTIVITES

The goals of the research activities are to: (1) relate Chapter 16 on an applied learning dimension, and (2) get you involved in research.

1. **Developing Futuristic Research Questions.** Develop five interesting research questions that are limited due to our lack of scientific tools, but for which we might have tools, and ultimately scientific answers, in the future.

2. **Is Science Value-Free? Cross Cultural Sexuality Research.** Research using InfoTrac how different cultures define and view homosexuality (e.g., Mexican culture versus African culture.

    Identify societal biases that you are aware of, related to homosexuality, as well as some of the biases inherent in your value system. Describe the influence that these biases may have on both your thinking and your ability to research homosexuality.

3.   **Diverse Explanations of Aggression**

What does science tells us about aggression? Use InfoTrac to research different theories about the causes of aggression. Include social, cultural, genetic, and evolutionary perspectives.

RESEARCH SUMMARY AND DISCUSSION QUESTIONS

Beyond Method

Ekman, P., & Friesen, W. V. (1971). Constants across cultures in the face and emotion. *Journal of Personality and Social Psychology, 17*, 124-129.

In Chapter 16, Ray emphasized the value of challenging our cultural worldview. This study by Ekman and Friesen demonstrated how cross cultural investigations can challenge our shared world view.

This study examined the universal meaning of facial expressions across cultures. Previous research conducted by Ekman and Friesen had found that the meaning of facial expressions across cultures was universal; however, their work was criticized because all of the participants in their studies had been exposed to facial expressions in the mass media. Their challenge was to conduct their research using people who had never been exposed to mass media.

The investigators traveled to New Guinea to conduct their study with people from a Fore tribe who lived an isolated Stone Age existence. None of these people had been exposed to the mass media. Fore adults and children were shown photographs of Westerners expressing various basic emotions (e.g., happiness, anger, disgust, fear, surprise). They were told stories in their own language and asked to identify the photographed facial expression that best matched the story. Ekman and Friesen found that the Fore people were very accurate in choosing the correct expression to match the story. In fact, there was no significant difference between Westerners and Fore people on the interpretation of facial expressions. Thus the investigators concluded that facial expressions of basic emotions were indeed universal.

Discussion Questions

1.   Discuss the obstacles that these scientists encountered.
2.   Discuss how the investigators attempted to use science as a means of transcendence.

SUGGESTED READING

Matsumoto, D. (1994). *Cultural influences on research methods and statistics.* Pacific Grove, CA: Brooks/Cole.

ANSWERS

Fill-in: Self Test
1. Active
2. Naturalistic
3. Ecological
4. Research program
5. Progressive
6. Degenerative
7. Multiple working hypotheses
8. Experience

True/False: Self Test
1. True
2. False
3. False
4. True
5. True
6. True
7. False
8. True
9. False
10. True

Multiple Choice: Self Test
1. D
2. B
3. A
4. D
5. B
6. D
7. C
8. A
9. D
10. D
11. A
12. D
13. D